Voices of Michigan
an Anthology of Michigan Authors

Volume Two
2000

~~~

Foreword by Kathy-jo Wargin,
a Michigan author.

Voices of Michigan
Mackinac Jane's Publishing Company
Box 475
Mackinac Island, Michigan 49757

Voices of Michigan
an Anthology of Michigan Authors
Volume Two

Second volume, 2000
First printing, May 2000
Copyright © 2000

Published in the United States of America by
MackinacJane's Publishing Company

Printed in the United States of America by
Thomson-Shore, Inc.
7300 West Joy Road
Dexter, Michigan 48130-9701

Library of Congress Catalog Number: 00-132096
ISBN: 0-9667363-1-1

Cover painting ~ Mary Hramiec-Hoffman
Pen and Ink Sketches ~ Karen R. James, Rob Harrell
Cover Design ~ Robert Roebuck
Typesetting ~ Juanita Smith
Editing ~ Janice Trollinger
Additional editing by Jane H. Winston

Voices of Michigan

MackinacJane's Publishing Company
Box 475
Mackinac Island, Michigan 49757

Voices of Michigan
an Anthology of Michigan Authors
Volume Two

is dedicated to

All Michigan residents who enjoy writing.

Acknowledgment

We sensed this project was going to be a success from day one. What we were not totally prepared for was just how successful the first volume was going to be! This is evidenced by the fact that we received 54% more manuscripts for the second contest than we did the first; we have had four times as many visits to our website this year as last year; we already have received manuscripts for the third volume. Another clear indicator of our success is the grand party we had on Mackinac Island last June honoring our winning authors. We anticipated 150 invited guests, so imagine our surprise and delight when the crowd swelled to over 400!

Clearly Michiganders enjoy writing and more importantly enjoy seeing their words in print. Being one of the vehicles that allows these emerging authors' dreams to come true is what gives us, the publishers of the anthology, so much pleasure.

Thanks to **Roman Barnwell** and **John Winston**, the faithful spouses of Mary Jane Barnwell and Jane Winston, the publishers. Thanks to **Juanita Smith**, the typist and **Janice Trollinger**, the editor. **Mary Hramiec-Hoffman's** painting and **Robert *Roebuck's*** skills as a graphic artist provide us with the perfect cover for volume two. **Karen Renae Jones** and **Rob Harrell's** pen and ink sketches provide the perfect transition from genre' to genre' throughout the book.

Without our readers to judge the contest, we would be nowhere, so a public thank you to: **David Abbey, Anne Beaty, Jerry Brown, Suzanne Davis, CT Duncan, Julie Foust, Linda Garner, Dorothy Hardman, Eileen Hoover, Cathy Kemp, Joan Maril, Jeaneene Nooney, Janet Rathke, Wini-Rider Young** and **Brett Van Emst.**

~Mary Jane Barnwell and Jane Winston

Foreword

by
Kathy-jo Wargin, a Michigan author

A little bit of the writer lives in us all. We may not always recognize it, but it's there. It is that little voice that provokes us to look a bit more closely at the magnificent and obscure things in life. It's that yearning to stall on a summer evening so we can watch a warm orange sunset suspend itself over the lake. It's the urge that drives us to dance around in the rain when no one is watching, and the echo of old familiar words as they fill our hearts and our minds prompting us to stand by the window on a cold winter day and look for diamonds in the snow.

It is a soulful feeling that makes us want to create images with our words, whether it's for a long lonely love letter or a really great list for the grocery store. It is there, and it has a pulse.

There is one trait, however, that separates those who write their thoughts and feelings for only themselves from those who write for the world to see - and that is courage.

It takes a brave heart to put something down on paper, to read it to your family, your friends, and then to hand it to a stranger and tell them sure, go ahead, please, please show it to the world.

I applaud these talented writers who, with warmth, honesty, creativity and courage are sharing their words, their thoughts - their souls - with the world. In **Voices of Michigan**, they are sharing their wonderful stories and poems so we all have a chance to enjoy their gifts. These are stories that will make us listen a bit more closely to the writers who exist in and around us all. I know you will enjoy these stories and thank these authors for making the world a little bit richer with their words, their hearts, and their stories - they are the truest voices of Michigan.

    ~Kathy-jo Wargin is the author of Michigan's Official State Children's Book, *The Legend of Sleeping Bear*, as well as *The Legend of Mackinac Island* and *Scenic Driving Michigan.* She also provided poems for *M is for Mitten, A Michigan Alphabet Book* and wrote the prose for the coffee table book, *Michigan, The Spirit of the Land,* which is a collection of photographs taken by her husband and professional partner Ed Wargin. Her latest book is *The Legend of the Loon.* Kathy-Jo lives with her family in northern Michigan.

Contest information

Voices of Michigan, n Anthology of Michigan Authors, is the product of a state-wide writing contest. All Michigan writers are urged to submit their poems, short stories or works of non-fiction to the refereed-contest. A select panel of judges read each of the entries, determine which are the best, and those authors are published in the anthology.

The entries need not be about Michigan, but the authors need to have Michigan ties. For more in-depth information on the contest, one can visit *Voices* website: www.voicesofmi.com, contact the publishers via email at macjanes@juno.com, write the publishers at *Voices of Michigan*, Box 475, Mackinac Island, Michigan or call 231.487.1098 and request the forms for the contest.

There is an entry fee and a contest entry form must be included with multiple copies of the work submitted.

KING OF THE NORTH WOODS

Voices of Michigan

Contents

Appendices:

FICTION

MASTERING THE FLY

1

Voices of Michigan

Beavers Fly

Tom Hoover

Lev Horchow was the last person I wanted to be out stomping around with in a cedar bog at the crack of dawn. The day was shaping up to be a typical late winter Michigan mixmaster of a day. Sleet then rain then drizzle then back to sleet again. And me out in the middle of it carrying a day pack weighed down with four slightly damp sticks of dynamite. The three of us, Lev, my neighbor Brian Sears, and I slogged along a trail paved with jack-pine trunks

Tom Hoover has lived in Michigan for 20 years having come from Kokomo, Indiana in a tiny boat full of Hoosier refuges. He lives with his wife, Eileen and daughter Zoe in a small house full of toys. His story *King of the Forest* was published in the inaugural edition of *Voices of Michigan*

and gravel. Following behind Brian, staring at his ridiculously colored Nautica jacket, I tried to reckon just how I got myself out here in the first place. It partly came down to me just trying to help out someone new to the island, but mostly I was just nosey. Brian had come up from Detroit and built a huge house down the road from mine. He was so young and so obviously rich that I got curious. What's a young guy with money enough to build a new home on an island like? Was he a criminal? Was he an heir to some vast fortune? I had to find out.

When Brian came to me with his tale of woe about how beavers were turning his 200 acres of prime north shore

wilderness beach front into an intractable swamp, I jumped at
the chance to show him how to solve the problem. The first
advice I gave him, over several glasses of scotch that he
poured from a decanter *not* a bottle, was to get a hold of Lev
Horchow. The second advice I gave him was to listen and to
do whatever Lev recommended, then I told him to stand a
good distance away while Lev did it.

Lev Horchow had been born on the island and was the
third and probably last of his line. Lev hadn't hooked up with
any sort of person willing to have anything to do with him
marriage-wise. Lev didn't wash and had exactly six and a half
teeth in his head. He was part drunk or full-blown drunk
twenty four hours a day. A lot of us couldn't imagine who or
what a life partner for Lev would be like. When you thought
of Lev, procreation never entered the picture. There were
people on the island willing to see to it that Lev and
procreation never became a reality. The idea was just too
horrible for them to contemplate.

Lev lived on a small island a hundred yards off shore
from the main island and was connected to the "mainland" by
a spit of land. Normally, this spit (Lev called it his driveway)
was a morass of sticky, freezing mud. Even at the height of
summer, with no rain, this access to Lev's place was a
quagmire of cool mud being air-conditioned by the wings of
billions of mosquitoes and deer flies.

Lev's home was two ancient Blue Bird busses
connected in the middle by a dilapidated Air Stream trailer
forming an "H"-shaped structure Lev called his compound.
The whole thing was painted in camouflage patterns of olive
drab, black and brown, and encircled by various sorts of snow
fencing that Lev had procured from the county road

commission garage over the course of many winters. When I first saw Lev's place, I jokingly referred to it as the architectural apex of the hovel. He laughed and laughed. He made me write down what I had said and for months afterwards, he repeated my description to anyone who'd listen. One time, down at the bar, I saw him struggle to remember my comment, give up, and spend a good minute drunkenly retrieving the piece of paper out of a pocket, a piece of paper that was about a year old by then.

Lev's compound was surrounded with the stuff he had spent thirty years collecting and tossing aside: canoes, speed boats, refrigerators, generators, snow mobiles, engine hoists, various eras of automobiles, and all manner of ambiguous metal implements. Off to the side of the compound was a large lean-to shed filled with old but working power tools of every kind. The shed was bound on one side by three broken chest freezers set in a row with their lids missing. These were filled to overflowing with empty beer cans. In Michigan you get a dime for every beer can you save and return. The freezers represented Lev's version of a rainy day bank account. When he ran short of cash, he'd bag up a freezer load and hitch the ferry into Cheboygan to cash his cans in at the Piggly Wiggly.

Lev only had to resort to this desperate measure in the lean winter months. Every other time of year, he was a busy man. All the summer people vacationing from down state came to rely on Lev's handyman expertise. If your septic guy was stumped by your gimpy sewer system, he'd more than likely defer the problem to Lev. The same went for any of the local electricians, carpenters, plumbers, and car mechanics. They all knew Lev as something of a mechanical genius, and they all owed him. His indispensable usefulness excused him from a multitude of sins, most of them alcohol related and some just related to Lev's particularly dark and squirmy bend of mind.

When Brian Sears offered Lev money up front to fix his beaver problem, he immediately became Brian's best friend in the world. He told Brian that getting rid of beavers would be no problem.

"Just gimme a week or so an' I'll be ready," he said. "And, hey, couldja gimme that down payment in cash? I got a little tax problem." Meaning he didn't pay taxes and the more pay under the table the better.

One day, after a particularly grueling night of drinking with Lev, Brian called me up to ask for some moral support and a little backup in the whole venture.

"I *trust* you and all, but Lev just isn't coming across to me as the 'can-do' type."

Brian spoke quietly over the phone; the sound of his own voice was causing his head to throb. I figured any minute the guy was going to bring up the money he put down. So I come out with it.

"How much you give him up front?"

"A hundred dollars."

I shook my head as I gazed out my front door. Down the road about half a mile away sat Brian's brand new house snug up against a two hundred foot stretch of beach made with the best sand that money could buy. Guys were busy putting the finishing touches on a huge steel and concrete boat dock. With the house and all, I figured I was looking at a million dollars easy. And Brian was about to start whining that Lev was wasting his hundred bucks. I sighed.

"Brian, that's about a week's pay for Lev. Don't give him any more. Stay home this week. Wait for him to call or come by. And don't go drinking with him. *Nobody* does that, and if you keep it up, it'll kill you."

Silence on the line for a second.

"Okay, but how do I check up on him...see that he's taking care of business?"

"The way it's done with Lev is no money up front, wait for him to come to you when he's ready, and don't plan on following a schedule. Hey, you got all summer."

I heard a sound on the line. A soft moan. Brian's unhappy sound.

"Actually, we don't. We got an architect coming next month to look at the land. We gotta pick a spot for the lodge we're gonna build. We *have* to get rid of those beavers soon, so the land can drain before my guy sees it."

I wanted to ask who this "we" was when I remembered this was how Brian referred to himself on occasion, like he was an organization or corporation all of his own. Which, I guess, he was.

"I'll talk to Lev for you. Get him moving. Just be ready. When Lev gets started you better be ready for some long days of work. He likes to start before sun up, so don't be surprised when he comes knockin'. And don't say anything about his drinkin' either."

I felt the beginning of a headache. Brian was going to be a problem.

"Well, okay, bud! I'll leave it up to you!" Brian said, perking up a bit. "Tell Lev to let me know soon. Oh! Would you be willing to join in? Help out, I mean? I'll pay you."

I closed my eyes, said a prayer, and hoped God would

remember this the next time I did something blasphemous.

"Sure, no problem. I want $75 a day, and I'll hold you to that, understand?"

"Great! Great! Thanks Jim! I feel lots better about this whole thing now. Let me know whenever you get news, 'kay?"

"Sure thing. Glad to make you feel better. Talk to you later. G'Bye."

So there it was; I was committed. I went around for the next couple of days avoiding Brian and half-heartedly looking for Lev. Late on a Saturday afternoon I was watching golf at the bar and trying to decide if I was going to go ahead and spend the rest of the day drinking or go home and drink while I patched my boat. It was a freezing damp March day and mucking around in my boat shed was looking less attractive with each passing Budweiser. The door slammed and I glanced over my shoulder just in time to see Lev careening toward me waving all of his limbs simultaneously and at different speeds. Lev was drunk, but with Lev it was always a matter of degree. It was late on a weekend, so Lev had probably finished his latest fix-it job and was just getting started. That meant he'd only had a six pack or a half pint and had, therefore, not lost the ability to speak English or recognize old friends like me. He hollered at me as he sauntered to the bar.

"Jimbo! Been lookin' all over for ya! I hear tell your gonna help out with Brian's beaver problem! I got a fool-proof method for getting' rid of the buggers, but I'm gonna need a steady hand like you ta help."

I opened my mouth to ask Lev what he was talking about when he reached over my shoulder and slammed a hundred dollar bill down so hard the bottles behind the bar rattled.

"Shorty! Gimme a short an' a shot an' one of whatever Jimbo's drinkin'! We got business ta discuss!' Lev hopped onto the stool next to me. He smelled of burnt axle grease and rotting vegetation. He was completely covered in a fine dusting of grime. When Shorty brought the drinks, Lev grabbed the tiny shot glass and tossed his down in one smooth stroke, a snake-like, fluid movement born of many years of practice. Lev tapped the bar for another one.

"I went out ta Brian's property and tramped around a little. Man! He's got one hell of a parcel out there! But it's *swamp*! I counted four lodges. Three small ones an' one tha's as wide as your house an' half as high."

I whistled appreciatively; I was familiar with what beavers could do, but this was something else altogether.

"I spent the week trappin' an' I got a dozen of the little bastards. Adults and little 'uns. I knocked over the small lodges an' got the land drainin' a bit. I set a stake in the middle o' the mess an' yesterday the water'd gone down a foot."

Shorty set down another shot , which Lev whisked into his mouth without skipping a beat.

"Trouble is the big lodge. Gonna need dy-no-mite! Only way! There's a big rogue male down deep in that lodge an' the damned thing's like Fort Knox. It's a god-DAMNED fortress!"

The three syllables, *dy-no-mite*, caught my immediate attention. Good sense told me to walk away from the whole operation. My heart, however, was telling me that I'd just gone through a long boring winter and that a little crazy

9

adventure was just the ticket to jump start my spring. *Dy-no-mite. Ho-lee cow.*

"So it's a fortress!" I said, tossing down my beer for emphasis. "It's not like the thing's gonna shoot at us or anything! What the hell we gotta mess around with dynamite for?"

Lev screwed up his rubber-mask face and growled at me.

"You ain't been listenin'! This beaver's gotta be 60 or 70 pounds! He's built a lodge that only a bulldozer could take down. Now, since I ain't willin' ta sink a dozer back there in Brian's swamp, the next thing we can do is blast the bugger out of there. YOU ever eradicated beaver before?"

I made some crack about my honeymoon and Lev cackled.

"Well, there ya go! Shorty! Get Jimbo another an' keep mine comin'!"

The rest of the day degenerated into the night which melted into unconsciousness and the bright pain of the next day. I was sitting at my kitchen table waiting for the water to boil when the phone rang. The noise made my hair hurt, and I gingerly pressed the receiver to my ear. It was Brian. He was cheerful and upbeat, talking fast. He was totally unaware that he was talking to someone near death.

"Jim? Hey, Lev dropped by this morning"...*This MORNING!*... "and he said that the constable was going down to a swap meet in Three Rivers tomorrow, so it'd be a perfect time to dynamite. He said he'd swing by about five tomorrow morning so' we could be done before noon. You want to meet me here, and we'll go out to the property in the Cruiser?"

10

I mumbled something approximately positive and hung up without saying goodbye. The water was boiling, but I shut it off and went back to bed. Making macaroni and cheese for lunch was beyond my capabilities. I needed bed rest. I needed a transfusion. I needed a reason to live. Blowing up beavers with dynamite the next day was just intriguing enough to give me the will to go on. I fell asleep, visions of explosions dancing in my head.

I woke up, startled by some subliminal alarm that told me I was missing something. What I was missing was most of a day. My internal clock had gone off like a bomb when it determined that I was not merely taking a nap but truly down for the count. I got up and frantically looked out the window. I was completely disoriented. It was too dark to see anything, but it was enough to tell me that I had indeed slept though the day. I looked at the clock. Three a.m.! Jesus! I'd slept through the day and was starting on another. I got dressed while I chanted to myself about never drinking with Lev Horchow again.

I was in the middle of making a four egg omelet when someone pounded of my kitchen door; I answered it brandishing an eight inch chef's knife.

"Hold on there, Jimbo! Don't stab you're ole drinkin' buddy! Mmmm! Smells good! Too bad we ain't got time ta eat! C'Mon! git cher coat! Let's hit the road!"

It was Lev. I caught a whiff of stale vodka and smoked chubs as Lev barged in, turning off my stove and grabbing the jacket from the back of my chair. He hustled me out the door like an old farm woman shooing chickens out of the yard.

"C'mon! let's git while the gittin's good! Hell! Brian was easier goin' than you!'

We got out in the yard, and in the morning twilight, I saw Brian sitting pie-eyed behind the wheel of his big Toyota. He didn't say anything; he just slammed the beast into gear and took off down the Perimeter road. We rode in peace for a bit. I was thinking about my omelet and trying to breathe in as little of Lev's effluence as possible. Brian drove like a fugitive on the run until Lev broke the silence.

"Say, Brian? It's your dime an' all, but if you keep drivin' like Mario Andretti, this dy-no-mite in my lap's gonna get us there faster'n anything Mario ever drove!"

Brian stood on the brakes.

"Holy cow! You got that stuff in HERE?" Brian said, fear creeping into his voice.

"Yeah! Where else am I gonna have it? Up my dress? Now, c'mon! I didn't mean for ya ta stop. Just take her easy an' don't rattle the bumps so hard. Hey, Jimbo! Take this!"

Lev handed me a small day pack. It was pretty heavy, and I took a peek inside. Four small brown cylinders. Dynamite. I felt the blood drain from my face. Somehow, illogically, I thought the stuff was safer when it had been in Lev's lap and not my own. Lev still had a pack in his lap.

"Lev, what's in your bag?" I asked, trying mightily to keep the quiver out of my voice.

"Oh, the blastin' caps, detonator, wire an' some more dy-no-mite."

"God, how much more?" Brian was driving slowly, all hunched over the wheel. I could tell he was homing in on our conversation.

"Four more sticks. I *told* you it was a damned big-assed lodge out there!"

"Well, couldn't you have split 'em up--leave some out

12

at the site--so we aren't carrying so much on us?"

Lev snorted derisively.

"Sheeit! Lemme tell ya what an old foreman tole me when I worked the quarry down in Utica! He tole me always ta carry enough dynamite ta kill ya! "Cause if ya didn't carry enough ta blow ya ta bits, then you'd wind up livin' as a cripple. I mean, what kinda life would that be? No arms or no legs...or even, God help ya, no tallywhacker! Either a you ever thought about *that*?"

I stared at Lev. For a second he had had me, until he said "tallywhacker." I hadn't heard anyone say "tallywhacker" since my long-dead Grandfather was alive. Brian and I both burst into gales of laughter. The world came back into focus, and Lev's little corner of reality went back into the weird jack-in-the-box that he uses for a mind. Lev was smart enough to know when he was being laughed at, and he sank back, sulking in his seat.

We went on in silence for a few more minutes until we came up on a small logging road cut off the main road. If you'd driven more than thirty, you'd have gone right by it, especially in the drizzling gloom we were driving through. We went up the road for about a half a mile when Lev suddenly came to life and told us to stop. We arranged our jackets, put on waders, and organized our gear. We headed out with Lev in the lead. There was little discussion. We were all business and wanting to get things done and get out of the weather. Brian didn't say a word about what the itinerary was going to be or how long it was going to take to get to the lodge. He was content to let Lev do the job he was hired to do.

We trudged along for the better part of an hour, and I was beginning to think that Lev had taken us the long way out just to teach us a lesson. It was pretty full light by the time we got to the lodge. It was surrounded by an oval shaped pond thirty yards at its widest point and about fifty yards long. All around that, including the land we stood on was a boggy mud basin punctuated, for as far as you could see, by vertical pointed sticks of varying thickness. Brian whistled low.

"*One* beaver did all this? In three weeks? Holy cow!"

Lev took a drink from his flask.

"Yeah, one beaver or a couple of really big bears...don't really know which."

Brian looked at me in alarm. I shrugged.

Lev had led us on a roundabout route; I could see the Cruiser sticking out of small stand of scrub maples a hundred yards from the other side of the beaver lodge. Lev had taken us in a huge circle. The vindictive little bastard. Lev grabbed my arm and started hauling me toward the lodge talking to Brian over his shoulder as we went.

"C'Mon, Jimbo! We'll lay some dy-no-mite while Brian here reconnoiters a good spot for shelter when we blow 'er. Make sure it's far away. Couple hunert yards oughta do it."

I scrambled after Lev as he waded toward the lodge. The thing was at least ten feet high and ten feet around, the size of a construction dump truck, the kind used to haul dirt away from foundation excavations. The beaver that built this lodge must be one magnificent member of his species. I immediately started hoping he wouldn't show up while we were busy blowing up his house. I must have been dawdling because Lev was yelling at me.

"C'Mon! Get a move on! I'm freezin' out here! Climb up this way!"

14

I found a hand-hold and pulled myself up onto the lodge. It was tough going because the thing was covered with wet, half-frozen mud, and Lev was offering no help at all. He was at the top of the mound with his ear on the surface listening. I struggled up to Lev and was about to ask if he heard anything when he popped up and grabbed the pack out of my hand.

"He's in there!" he whispered, the frozen mist of his breath reeked of vodka. "Let's get this laid out quick before he leaves! I'll lay the sticks an' you follow with the wire...try not to tangle it up or tighten the slack. Just let the wire lie loose. Now, follow me close!"

We went around and around the lodge in a more or less spiraling fashion until we ended up in the water at our starting point. I didn't do much because after I fumbled the first two connections, Lev grabbed the wire from me and had me follow him with the caps and dynamite.

"You're yankin' on it like it was a one tit cow!" He yelled.

At some points he'd mutter to himself and giggle a little. Once or twice he changed the position of a stick of dynamite whispering to himself,... *"Yeah, yeah, here! Better boom! Go straight up!"*

Finally, after what seemed like an hour, we waded back to semi-dry land to look for Brian. He was daintily smoking a Kool as he crouched behind a small stand of birches. It didn't look like it was far enough away to me, but Lev nodded approval. The wind was picking up, and light snow was starting to spit from the sky. I was freezing and wet and ready to get this thing done.

Lev screwed the ends of the Prima-Cord wire to the

detonator and handed the thing to Brian who looked at it with a blank expression.

"There ya go, Brian!" Lev shouted above the wind. "It's your land! Do the honors!"

Brian looked at me searching for guidance. I made a twisting motion with my hands and shouted.

"Turn the handle!...Twist it!"

"You mean now?"

"YES!" Lev and I shouted in unison.

Brian yanked on the detonator. The flash and the sound crushed us all to the ground. I landed in a mud puddle and stuck there. I was starting to think that it really *was* too much dynamite after all when Lev ran across my face, totally unhinging my train of thought.

"Run!" he screamed. "Run before all that shit lands on us!"

Instinctively, I looked up, and from there on the ground I had a perfect view of the beaver's lodge from underneath as it came screaming back down from the sky. My mind caught up with my body about the time I was trying to scramble over Lev's back to get away. Lev shook me off and we wrestled with each other until we got to the car. We each hit a door and looked back to see if Brian had followed. He was standing stock still, looking straight up, transfixed. Both of us screamed at him, but he wouldn't budge. I looked at the sky and spotted a small object separating itself from the mass of dirt, wood, and muck hurtling right for Brian. It was two oval shapes stuck together end-to-end. As the thing got closer, it coalesced into a shape with color and movement. A second later it became a smoldering, bewildered beaver careening toward Brian with the accuracy of a heat-seeking missile. I screamed at Brian to move, but he was frozen by the vision of a hassock-sized, burning mammal zeroing in on him from out of the sky. He yelled something right before the thing hit, but the wind whipped his words away. The beaver hit him full in the face with a sound like wet sand bags hitting pavement from a height. Then the rest of the lodge rained down for about ten seconds. Give Lev credit; the thing did go straight up and it came straight down, completely destroyed. And now Mr. Beaver was, presumably, in heaven chewing down God's green acre of trees; wondering how he got there and why all of his fur was burned off. Lev, struck with the revelation that his meal ticket might be dead, or worse yet, unable to pay up, ran straight back to Brian. I got there in time to see Brian come to long enough to look at Lev and say, "You're fired!" before he passed out. Lev cursed and yelled at me to help carry him.

We drove back to Brian's house trying to figure out what to do all the way there. Brian was sprawled in the back, whimpering and moaning. When we pulled into his drive, he came alive and started yelling at Lev.

"Jeeezus! You could have killed me! You miserable little shit! And YOU! You were supposed to protect my investment! You didn't tell us the damn things could fly! You didn't tell us that's what this freak had in mind! I think the thing broke my nose! Keeerist! Beavers flying! What the hell am I supposed to do about that? Huh? Who was supposed to warn us about that, huh? YOU, good neighbor? Get the hell out of my car!"

Lev got out and went around to help Brian, but he was already out and screaming at Lev, who stood impassive, looking through Brian as he went on and on. I got out and walked to my house, the sound of Brian's yelling receding in the damp mid-morning air.

Lev eventually did get paid. The water dried up, and about a year later, Brian had his lodge up and running. It was a success from the day it opened. Brian only spoke to me when he absolutely had to, and that was just about never. Lev hasn't changed. He still fixes the unfixable. Brian spent a night in jail over the winter because of Lev. During the dinner hour at the bar, a spectacularly drunk Lev had suggested to a table full of Brian's friends that the lodge be called "The Flying Beaver." I thought it was a perfectly good suggestion, but Brian didn't take it well. He cracked Lev over the head two or three times with a pool cue before the constable knocked Brian down and put a foot on his neck. Lev didn't press charges. He told me later it just wasn't worth it.

"I mean, lookit," Lev told me. "After a guy's been plastered in the head by a flyin' beaver, he just ain't ever gonna be normal like you an' me. Nosir! Poor bastard's gonna have ta take that vision with 'im the rest of his life. Think about it! A flamin', stinkin' beaver right in the kisser! Goddamned horrible! Ole Brian ain't ever gonna be right. Gonna go through life lookin' up at clouds an' flinchin' every time! Hell, if it was me, I'd never look up. Yeah. Flyin' beaver'll mess you up. Change your life. An' not for the good neither!"

I nodded my head, ordered another round, and pondered Lev's wisdom. But I didn't ponder very long or very hard.

Stone Throw Cottage: Betsy's Story

Chris F. Hauge

The ferry...

The ferry ride across Lake Huron from Mackinaw City to Mackinac Island is everything Betsy described in our treatment sessions. The ferry left its Mackinaw City berth promptly at 1900. I smile to myself. Strange, since Viet Nam, how much I hate the military, but I still think and write in military time.

The clouds behind Mackinac bridge split into a V-shaped canyon allowing only a silver, gold and blue backdrop to frame the bridge, an almost spiritual painting in the evening sky. In contrast, the muffled roar of the ferry's engines triggers an unwanted flashback to the gun boats in Viet Nam. Fortunately, that memory is broken by the voice on the loud speaker beginning to extol the wonders of Mackinac Island.

"Grand Hotel." I remember Betsy insisting, "Lance, it is not *the* Grand Hotel; it is Grand Hotel. Only the tourists refer to it as The Grand Hotel." It seems important that I come to her island as a resident, not a summertime visitor.

Dr. Chris F. Hauge is retired from the United States Air Force. He and his wife Sally live in Wilmington, North Carolina where Chris has his own psychotherapy private practice and serves as an adjunct professor at two Universities. This is his first fiction contest, and he has plans to do much more writing

19

"Fort Mackinac and The Tea Room. The Governor of Michigan's Summer Residence. Marquette Park and Windermere Point." I know that just around Windermere Point, I will be at Stone Throw Cottage. Because of hearing hours of Betsy's terse, but engulfing, description of living on her island, I am not arriving as a stranger. She could capture all five senses in a few words.

The loud speaker voice fades to background, and I am aware only of the cool touch of the urn I am holding carefully in my lap. Like her stinginess with words in life, Betsy wanted nothing elaborate in her death. She picked out the urn in Wilmington as soon as she knew she had only months to live. She brought the urn to me in one of our sessions with detailed instructions for her cremation. "No dead body to stare at and no maudlin memorial service!" With that, Betsy handed...more like tossed...me the deed and keys to Stone Throw Cottage. Without ever having seen Stone Throw, I can see it in my mind in exquisite detail. It is as though I had grown up with it as Betsy had.

Now I can see the long white porch of Grand Hotel to the left, the umbrellas of the Tea Room dead ahead with the turn-of-the-century, colorful hotels and houses of the island at their feet. The Captain throttles back, easing the ferry into its dock.

Stone Throw Cottage...

The walk down Lakeshore Road takes me past the hotels, businesses, fudge and ice cream shops Betsy loved and helped me to see. Her urn is tucked safely under one arm and my overnight bag balances the other arm as I head toward

Windermere Point.

   I imagine Betsy holding my hand and dragging me in her excitement to be back and share her island with me as we walk. I can hear her describing the smells and sights and sounds as she had so often in my office. It is as if she is here, walking, skipping with me.

   Even in death, Betsy can still command my attention. "Look there! That's a horse-drawn carriage tour. And there's a dray. Everything comes to the island by ferry boat to that dock down there and then has to be loaded on the drays and be delivered. Even the taxi is horse-drawn. Take a deep breath, Vance." She invites me. "Smell the horse shit? I call it Street Fudge. It's really fresh and alive, isn't it?" Betsy's right. Although I had never smelled manure in those terms, it is a fresh, clean smell. "See that guy cleaning up the street?" She points to a man in orange coveralls with a shovel, broom and push cart. "They do that all day. Early in the morning, you can come downtown and the street is washed. It is so fresh and wet and cool with the sun just rising." She can hardly contain the excitement in her voice. I vow to take in that experience. "Smell those lilacs, will you?" I find myself burying my face in a tree of lilacs tumbling over a white picket fence in a brilliant purple and green cascade. "The very best lilac trees are right in front of Stone Throw. You'll see." Her enthusiasm is childlike, as though she was seeing the island for the first time.

   Betsy has let go of my hand, and I can see her walking backwards, taking in deep breaths and using all her senses, inviting me to lose myself in the beauty of her island. Her eyes are delft-china blue and glisten with excitement. Betsy

21

is again the beautiful, slender, long-legged 21-year-old who
first came into my Group Therapy Class at the University of
North Carolina at Wilmington five years ago and immediately
took the hot-seat in a Gestalt Therapy demonstration the first
day of class. That day I had my introduction to just how
gutsy she was. My reverie is interrupted by the reality of the
clip clop of horses and the cool feel of the urn beneath my
arm. I am crying.

    I round Windermere Point, go past the Library and
several more colorful, large homes with lilacs and pools of
poppies and other flowers I haven't seen in North Carolina.
Immediately, I recognize Stone Throw Cottage: A Victorian,
two-story with a front porch across its width inviting you to sit
in the evening and chat with everyone who walks the
boardwalk on the shore of Lake Huron. The view from the
porch stretches out into the lake to the lighthouse on the left
and Mackinac Bridge on the right. The cottage itself is pale
blue. The porch, columns, front steps, and railings are light
gray. The entire corner lot is surrounded by a white picket
fence. As I open the front gate, I am greeted with well
defined, mounded flower gardens in front of the porch and on
either side of the worn, uneven, cement walk. In the corner
of one of the gardens is a rock garden filled with all sizes of
smooth white rocks taken from the beach and obviously
placed with great care. On each stone I can see writing,
some with just names and dates and some with longer
thoughts and memories of wonderful times spent here.

    As I sit on the top step and set the urn carefully beside
me, in my mind, Betsy is sitting cross-legged on the grass
beside the rock garden. "My grandparents built this cottage

around 1900." I can see her lovingly pick up one of the stones and carefully brush earth from it. "Each time someone visits the cottage, they are asked to walk about on the beach and allow a stone to choose them and then write something on it and put their stone in this garden." She looks up and the slowly setting sun just catches her dark, short-cropped hair as she puts the rock back in its place and points to one of the smaller rocks in the front of the garden. "That's my rock." Tears are welling in her eyes. "Daddy and I went out and picked that stone from the beach." She is looking toward Lake Huron. "Then he brought it up and he wrote my name, the date, and 'I love you' on it and put it right here. It hasn't been moved since. That was the last summer I spent with Daddy. After that he went back to Viet Nam and was killed during the evacuation of Saigon." Her voice trails off to a whisper. "But I told you all that before, didn't I?" She had told me about her father who was a physician in the Marine Corp. and was killed in Viet Nam. And she had also told me about the rock tradition and her rock. Now it is all so much more vivid sitting on the worn, gray steps of Stone Throw Cottage.

Suddenly, I see Betsy on her feet gesturing for me to follow her out the gate, across the road to the boardwalk at the edge of Lake Huron. I am sitting with my feet hanging over the edge with her urn beside me, the sun still clinging to the day, but slipping behind the bridge. It is late, but still a golden twilight. I see Betsy beside me again. She gestures to the infinite array of white, washed rocks of all shapes and sizes stretching out into the lake. "This is how my grandparents named the cottage Stone Throw. Go ahead, pick out some

23

stones and skip them on the lake. This is the best place on the island to find and skip stones."

I am gingerly picking my way across a beach of stones, choosing the perfect, small, oblong, flat ones and skipping them into Lake Huron. I find myself laughing out loud. "God, Betsy, I haven't done this since I was a snot-nosed kid at the lake in Minnesota." In my mind I hear Betsy's laugh.

"Hey, Lance, you're pretty good at skipping stones for a 52 year old fart." Two gulls are flying into the lingering, gold sunset. Betsy looks up and smiles at the pair as they are lost in the distance.

Island Child...

"May I take some pictures of your lilacs?" A tourist couple interrupts my stone skipping. "You bet, help yourself." I gesture toward the corner of the fence. Still difficult to believe they are "my lilacs." Sitting on the porch of Stone Throw as the sun is finally letting go, I am taken back to the porch of my home in the Historic District of downtown Wilmington, North Carolina. When Betsy came into my office for the first time, she seemed even taller and more statuesque than I remembered her from that first meeting in my class nine years earlier. The same soft, blue eyes, short, dark hair, angular face and slender figure not hidden at all in blue jeans and loose white shirt. She curled up in the easy chair and in her typical, terse fashion told me precisely why she was there.

"Doc, I'm dying of AIDS." Betsy is looking intently into my eyes for any sign of my flinching. I was struck by the fact that there were no visible effects of the virus. "I am refusing any drugs including AZT because I know there is no hope. I want to experience my own death and record it. I need your help. Maybe it'll help someone else to face the inevitable without all the bull shit. I am _not_ going out like a zombie on a salad bar of drugs! I even quit smoking pot because it dulls my senses. I remember you from those classes in group and gestalt therapy. When I took the hot seat, you really helped me finish a lot of old business with my mother. I know you don't believe in drugs. Neither do I, but I do need some help with the pain and I know you do hypnosis." Another intense search into me eyes. "Are you with me?"

After taking a moment to absorb all that, I knew I would treat Betsy, but I needed to respond to her intensity. "I thought you considered hypnosis to be glorified witchcraft."

"Still do, but it may be my only game in town." Betsy never lost eye contact.

Once I agreed to work with her, I spent hours fascinated with her strength and all she had accomplished since meeting her in my class.

"I am a product of growing up on two islands and riding ferries to and from the mainland. Summers on Mackinac Island. Winters on Bald Head Island off the coast of North Carolina. My Daddy was stationed at Camp Lejeune, North Carolina, and bought the place on Bald Head when I was a baby." She frowns. "For some reason, I never liked it there. I went to school by taking the ferry every day between Bald Head and the schools in Southport. Graduated from High School in the Spring of 1985." Her eyes hardened, but she didn't miss a breath. "I had been dating a guy named

25

Gary since my junior year. Just before our graduation, and I was about to leave for Mackinac Island, the son-of-a-bitch date-raped me." Then, only a hint of tears. "That summer, my mother killed herself on Bald Head. She just walked out into the ocean and cut both arms from her elbow to the palm. She was a nurse, so she knew how to do it." Tears were now becoming harder to dam back. "For God's sake, I was 17 years old and both my parents were dead." That was the last I saw Betsy cry. She wiped her tears with her sleeve and smiled. "There's one thing about both parents dead. You grow up quick, and there's no pressure to produce grandchildren." Betsy unfolded her long legs and stood. "Mind if I smoke, Doc?" I did, but I shook my head and she took out a thin cigar and lighted it. She smiled. "Guess lung cancer is the least of my worries now, eh?"

It took a while, but I finally asked if Betsy had any idea why her mother would choose that time to kill herself.

"She hadn't been herself since Daddy was killed." A long draw on the cigar. "I think my being raped pushed her over the edge. Mother really _did_ believe that good girls shouldn't get themselves raped. In any case, it was after I tried to talk to her. That summer I went to my island alone for the first time." After pausing, she smiles. "On the bright side, I own two very expensive pieces of property. Got my Bachelor's in Psychology at UNCW, my Master's and Ph.D. in Experimental Psychology from the University of Michigan, and did one year post-graduate work at Oxford in England, mostly because Daddy was a war hero." She puts the cigar out in a saucer I had managed to find for her. "Then the proverbial ax fell."

I asked her, "How did the ax fall, Betsy?"

She settled back into the easy chair and folded her legs beneath her. "I believe you know Kindra. She and I were roommates in Wilmington for four years. She graduated as an RN from UNCW. Kindra recommended you because she's been seeing you in therapy. She is a survivor of sexual abuse. You come highly recommended, Doc." Again she smiles and lights another small cigar and takes that first, deep draw on it. "I was finishing my post-graduate work in England when Kindra called me. As you know, she is working in a Hospice here in Wilmington. It seems Gary, the SOB who date raped me, checked into the Hospice with AIDS and checked out dead. I tested positive. He raped me in 1985 and it's '94. You do the math, Doc. That's nine years. I knew something was going wrong the year I was in England, but either it didn't occur to me to get tested, or I simply didn't want to know. Now I'm 26 years old. Worked my ass off to be called 'Doctor' and finally get started being a _real_ psychologist. I have two expensive homes and in the end, what does it matter? In a few months I'm dead. Not my finest year, eh?"

Elizabeth...

Like all victims of sexual abuse, Betsy was an excellent subject for deep hypnosis and age- regression. Her safe place was the porch and front steps of Stone Throw either at sunset or sunrise. It was on these steps we first met 11 year old Elizabeth, Betsy's Spiritual Core. From that first meeting to the last hypnosis as Betsy died, each age- regression and past-life experience began by meeting Elizabeth on the front steps of Stone Throw and ended by returning to the steps and front

27

porch.

Betsy's breathing was deep and regular as she sank deeper into the recliner and into trance. "I'm floating above watching myself sit down on the top step of the front porch at Stone Throw. It's hazy over Lake Huron at one of those never-ending twilights."

"Is there anyone with you?" I ask.

Betsy's voice is soft and her words come slowly, broken into partial sentences with long pauses between every word or two. "At first no…but I see Elizabeth… at the banister… to my right now."

I match my voice to the softness of hers. "Good, just let the scene develop now."

Then her words begin flowing effortlessly. "It doesn't seem right to just sit on the steps. I want to go down and sit on the boardwalk and skip some stones. At first Elizabeth doesn't want to come with me. Now she does and we go down to the boardwalk and she sits next to me. She's swinging her legs and kind of bouncing herself up and down. The breeze is blowing off the haze over the lake. I look back and the cottage seems far away. I can see it, but far and tiny in the distance. I ask Elizabeth where we are now. She tells me we are in the middle of my imagination. I ask her what we can do here. She replies, 'Anything you want.' I'm asking her if this is what it will be like when I die. Elizabeth smiles and takes my hand and tells me, 'If that is what you want then you can come here.' I tell her that I want to know about my past. There is so much I don't remember. Elizabeth continues to smile, squeezes my hand and tells me, 'Of course

28

you do. It's all here...I have it here for you.' She pats the boardwalk with her other hand. I am noticing how small her hand is in mine, yet how powerful she is. 'For you to get to the point where you know everything you want to, you will have to die. To know your past in this life is easy. To understand and know *all* your past lives you will have to surrender this life. It won't be long now.' Elizabeth smiles and gently squeezes my hand. Somehow knowing from Elizabeth that it won't be long, my death is no longer frightening."

Betsy opens her eyes one last time and smiles as she looks at me beside her, squeezes my hand and closes her eyes.

Daddy...

As the sun is finally surrendering to dusk, I am reading the letter Betsy wrote to her father just before she died. I suggested that she not worry about punctuation or spelling, but her precise writing was as much a part of her as her terse, blunt speech.

Dear Daddy,   May 1995

How do I deal with something that has been buried for 22 years because I couldn't remember? I'll tell you how. I own up to the fact that I *am* going to die! Not die in the existential sense, but die for real in the next few days! But I think you knew that when you went to Viet Nam and got *your* ass killed in 1973.

Daddy, I finally know why I always hated the place on Bald Head Island and loved and felt so safe in Stone Throw Cottage. I could always remember the warm, loving times

29

with you at Stone Throw for the first five years of my life. I could not remember until now how you violated my boundaries and used my body that last week we were together on Bald Head before you went back to Viet Nam.

Daddy, you told me not to tell anyone because you kept saying I enjoyed what you were doing to me. You said you were teaching me. Daddy, it hurt bad physically. You _had_ to know how much you were hurting me. But even more, because of what you did, I lost my life until now. And now I'm about to die. I lost my trust and then I lost you. For five years I trusted you, loved you. God how I loved and looked up to you. Then you scarred me for 22 years of my life, right to my death.

For what you did to me, I will not forgive you and I know you never forgave yourself. For being my Daddy and giving all you could, I love you and I can forgive you. I _have_ to forgive you because in that forgiveness I let go of all the shame and guilt and rage I have been stuffing all these years.

I will not see you after I die. I no longer believe in that myth. I am prepared to leave his life and begin another as I know I have done in many lives before.

I love you Daddy and hope you have continued your pilgrimage of soul as I will.

Love Forever, Betsy

I have fallen asleep on the porch. The sun is rising behind the light house in the Straits of Mackinac as I fold the yellow, legal-size page and pick up the urn.

Walking to the boardwalk in the early morning sun with Betsy's urn in both hands, I know that she didn't get to

write her letters to her mother or to that desperately hurting
five year old, child-within. She died a few hours after
finishing the letter to her father. I knew she wanted to tell
her mother that she finally understood that her mother took
her own life not because she lost her husband to Viet Nam all
those years ago. Not because her daughter had been raped.
Betsy finally understood that her mother choose to die
because she could no longer bury the pain of knowing that she
had never been able to be there for Betsy. With that
understanding, Betsy forgave her mother.

The Beginning...

At the end, Betsy was in the hypnosis chair. We both
knew these were the moments we had both worked toward
and prepared for. I pulled my chair close to her and gently
touched her cheek.

"Betsy, as you feel the touch of my fingers on your
face, your whole body is heavy and relaxed. As I count down
from 10 to 0, all feeling will leave your body. You will leave
the steps of Stone Throw with Elizabeth and your five year old
and walk to the boardwalk. When you're there, just smile."

Almost immediately a radiant smile engulfs her face.
I am having trouble concealing the tears in my voice.

"Beautiful. Now, as Stone Throw fades into the mist
behind you, you are there in the middle of your own
imagination with Elizabeth and your five year old. Say
goodbye to your five year old. Comfort her and tell her all
that you need to. Hold her once more. Now, gently let her
go." A long pause and Betsy slowly wraps her arms around

herself and again the beautiful, radiant smile. I know that Betsy has united with her five year old and then released her. "It's OK to go now, Betsy. I love you!" I can feel Betsy let go. Tears of joy are streaming down my cheeks.

I open the urn and allow the contents to float to the rocks below. The sun is still just behind the light house and I can see three perfect skipping stones at my feet. After throwing the urn as far into Lake Huron as I can, I pick up the three stones and skip them, one at a time, over the blue water dancing with gold sunlight. I am laughing out loud and sobbing at the same time. I have never skipped stones that far before.

Overhead three gulls glide effortlessly, noisily into the sun rise.

I am going to go downtown, smell the street fudge and the newly washed streets and get to know my island.

A Fine Day for Varmint Hunting

Laura Propp

Peering through the scope on the rifle, Cherie's head was perfectly centered and one finger movement away from death. Jeff flicked the safety back on and lowered the rifle. He heard the screen door squawk again, then Cherie swearing under her breath as the door slammed back shut.

"Jeff, are you home? I need some help with these groceries."

Jeff slipped his shoes off and proceeded to pad down the stairs in his stocking feet.

"Sorry, Hon, no can do. I'll ruin my socks."

Cherie stared hard at the back of Jeff's head as he rummaged through the first bag she'd brought in. She could feel the anger building already, and she hadn't been home five minutes. Fine, she'd do it herself.

She headed back for more of the grocery bags, sharply pulling the screen door shut despite the springs that brought it closed automatically.

Jeff smiled as the door slammed. He tore open a new bag of chips, munching and dropping crumbs all the way to

Laura and Steven **Propp** have been married for 20 years and have two handsome sons, Daniel and Robert. She enjoys reading, writing and vacationing at their cabin in Federic, Michigan. Squirrel fear her during hunting season! Laura recently found her father after 39 years, via the i n t e r n e t .

33

the fridge. She probably expected him to help her put the crap away. Wrong. He had other things on his mind. Jeff popped the top off the beer bottle, letting it fall on the floor, belched in Cherie's face as she came back in the house, her arms loaded with groceries, and headed back up the stairs.

Cherie watched his retreat with relief. She needed time to set her plans in motion.

She opened the fridge to put the milk away, thinking about the night she had met Jeff. Last Christmas her friend Kim, who worked for a marketing firm in Chicago, had coaxed Cherie into attending her company Christmas party with her. Free drinks, food and a little holiday spirit couldn't hurt, she remembered thinking.

Oh, but it had.

Jeff had come in with the catering service and made himself at home, pretending to be a guest. He had latched onto Cherie right from the beginning. She had been standing in front of the appetizers, contemplating the ham roll-ups, when someone bumped her arm from behind. The champagne glass tipped sideways just enough for her drink to slosh out onto her borrowed dress.

"Oh, excuse me; I'm sorry; did I do that?" Cherie remembered looking up into Jeff's face as he stood over her apologizing, his eyebrows furrowed together in concern. The intensity of his stare made her look away.

"Umm, no problem. The dry cleaners can probably take care of it," she mumbled as she wiped at her wet sleeve.

"The dress will survive. I'll get you another drink and some snacks. Sit here."

Jeff gripped her elbow firmly and took the nearly

empty glass out of her hand. He led her to a sofa away from the food table and the party crowd.

She should have had a clue right then. Jeff had started from the beginning telling her what to think and eat and how to act. She had still been in mourning for Kevin, her husband of 12 years, who had been killed in a freak car accident on Halloween. Though she had their daughter Jenny to take care of, she had still been lonely. When Jeff brought her another glass of champagne, he'd sat too close. She hadn't felt ready for romance, but after a couple more drinks, she began to feel flattered by the attention. Her memory was a little fuzzy after that. It was only later that she realized she had done all the talking and knew very little about him. She remembered Jeff telling her that her friend Kim had left with another man, and he offered to take her home. As her eyes had scanned the crowded room looking for Kim, she felt her head swoon. She'd thought it better to accept his offer and leave the party.

Cherie stepped off the bottom step of the porch and bent to pick up several beer bottle tops off the ground. Jeff always threw them down wherever he happened to be when he drank. She looked out into the yard and became distracted by another one of Jeff's unfinished projects. The grass in the middle of the circle drive was beginning to die around the edge of a huge mound of dirt and stones. Idly, she wondered what Jeff was going to do with it. He'd had the stuff delivered last week, and there it sat. He hadn't said, but she was sure if it involved work, he wouldn't finish it.

Cherie crawled into the van to retrieve the bottles of pop that had rolled to the back during the trip home. Her back ached, so she sat on the floor, wrapped her arms around her legs, and rested her chin on her knees, trying to remember what had happened when he brought her home that night. She closed her eyes.

He had walked her to the porch, taking the keys out of her hand and unlocked the door. She knew now that he intentionally had not given them back.

The blaring sound of Saturday morning cartoons had forced her out of bed the next morning. She'd focused her eyes on the clock, staring with disbelief as she had read 7:05. Her head was splitting from the unknown amount of champagne she had consumed, and her stomach threatened rebellion as she staggered to the bathroom. How did Jenny get home so early ?

She heard a man's laugh.

It wasn't Jenny.

Cherie remembered feeling threatened, even with the throbbing hangover. It was a deep sense of something waiting. She had thought at the time it was her drunken imagination playing tricks on her, but it had been Jeff.

Jeff stood in the upstairs window, watching the van, waiting for Cherie to come back out. What the hell was she doing? He finished off the beer and picked the rifle up. Releasing the safety, he peered through the scope looking for Cherie. He could make out her legs and feet and a part of her hands, clasped around her legs as though she were sitting in the van, waiting. Had she seen him in the window when she came in? Jeff doubted it. He watched her feet through the scope. I could put just one in the top of her foot and get the whole business rolling, he thought. He lowered the gun, shifting the safety back on. Better to stick to the original plan, he thought. She'd start screaming and someone would show up that wasn't in his plans, and then he'd have to kill the whole town. Best to wait.

He pulled the curtain back again, this time without the gun. He could still see her sitting there. What the hell was she doing?

Cherie reached for the bottles, rolling back on her heels as she hefted them forward to the open door of the van. Backing out, she thought about the premonition she'd had that Saturday morning, nearly two years ago.

It had been Jeff, not her daughter, Jenny, watching the cartoons that morning. He had been sitting in the good Lazy Boy in the front living room, laughing as the black and white Moe hit Curly in the head with a hammer. When he realized she was standing in the doorway, he'd jumped out of the chair, slid his arms softly around her waist, and hugged her. He had been tender and solicitous, pushing her hair back from her face and smiling into her eyes. Her sense of danger faded into tired relief. She had thought his concern was genuine. Now she knew it had all been a facade. Jeff had carefully constructed each conversation and the many intimate moments that would bring her under his control during the first months of their relationship.

Cherie remembered asking him how he got in. He had grinned sheepishly, acting embarrassed and replied that he had accidentally put her keys in his pocket the night before. He said he had wanted to get them back to her first thing that morning, but he knew she'd probably needed to sleep off the champagne, so he hadn't disturbed her. He figured he would just watch cartoons until she got up. He'd said he was concerned about her. There had been no sign of a hangover on him. His tan face, eyes gazing down at her, had looked good. She remembered thinking how fresh he had seemed, clothes neatly pressed, a light scent of Old Spice lingering in the air. It had been what her dad used when he was alive. The memory had given her a false sense of normalcy. She'd thought Jeff would be okay based on his cologne. She didn't remember reminiscing about her dad at the party, and how the smell of Old Spice always reminded her of him. It had been another one of Jeff's tricks. On his way home from dropping her off, he had stopped by the E-Z Mart and picked up a bottle. He never used cologne. Cherie figured it out later, after she found the unopened bottle she had given him for his birthday in the trash. Now, many months and bruises later, she would be the one with the trick up her sleeve. He thought she was stupid. He was wrong.

Holding the bag with the eggs in one arm, Cherie sat the liters of pop, a bag of potatoes and the last bag of groceries on the ground. As she bent to pick up the other bag of groceries, she looked up at the house, sensing rather than seeing Jeff's presence in the window. He thought she didn't know he was watching her.

He watched her ceaselessly.

Jeff stood watch at the window. He remembered why he'd chosen Cherie to persecute as he watched her shapely ass back out of the van. She had reminded him of the lady who used to live next door when he was a kid. Sheila was blond and built, despite the fact she'd popped out three kids. Jeff's second story room had faced the side of her house, so he'd had a front row seat to whatever went on, particularly if someone left the curtains open. Good ole Sheila. Man! She was fun to torment. Jeff remembered the first time he got her. She liked to sunbathe in the backyard, lying on her stomach with her top undone. One day he loaded the BB gun and plinked her in the ass from his window. The surprise hit had made her sit straight up, bare boobs hanging everywhere as she rubbed the spot he had hit. She must have thought a bee stung her because, two days later, she was back out in the yard, sunning herself. Jeff could feel himself getting excited thinking about it. Time to hit Cherie.

Cherie started for the house. Through the screen door, she could see the bottom stairs inside the house. The old farmhouse stairs were quiet except for the creak on the last step coming down. She heard rather than saw Jeff's feet coming off the stairs. Shoeless, his descent had been quiet until the creak on the bottom stair. As she climbed the porch stairs, her legs felt like sandbags, and she could feel her heart starting to beat faster in her chest. Something was up; she could feel it. Jeff was coming through the foyer, towards her. She stopped in front of the screen door, shifting each bag of groceries more securely onto each hip. Cherie braced herself.

"What the hell are you doing out here! You planning to cook dinner sometime today! And where's that lazy rugrat of yours? I told you yesterday I had shit for her to do."

Jeff's face scowled with rage, his arms spread out like a minister on Sunday when he preached on hell; his hands gripped the top of the door frame. The way his neck stretched forward, oddly, made Cherie think of a buzzard. She felt the sand flowing out of her legs, as they weakened. She hadn't anticipated having her plan in motion this soon.

"She stayed at her friend's house last night. I didn't know you wanted her."

Jeff plastered his face against the screen and began to scream.

"Do not tell me you did not know, you lying witch; the whole damn county heard me from the window last night. I cannot believe you are standing there and lying bare-faced to me!"

Cherie paled, knowing something was going to happen. Jeff enunciated each word when he was preparing to fight. This time was no different.

She watched as he pushed his face so hard against the screen, that he popped a corner off the door frame. He punched his arm through and shoved Cherie backwards. Cherie tried to shift sideways to avoid falling backward down the stairs and lost one bag of groceries in the process. Half a dozen cans of ravioli fell out of the bag, rolling with the tilt of the old farmhouse porch, disappearing off the edge, one by one. Cherie threw her free arm out, catching the bannister pole before she flipped backward over the rail. Miraculously, she held on, even hanging onto the bag with the eggs.

Jeff disappeared.

She leaned her head back against the post, trying to catch her breath and not cry. She hugged the remaining bag of groceries close, carefully opening the screen door. She heard the toilet flush, and she knew she had a minute to get to the back door.

Jeff came out of the bathroom and stood watching the kitchen door swing after Cherie. He had her scared, and she always played his games better in that frame of mind. Perfect. Yessiree, ladies and gentlemen, step right up and watch as the great Cherie LaFevre performs her grand finale. No admission charge. This would be a private viewing only. Jeff snickered silently at his pun. Too bad there wasn't someone here that enjoyed his terrific sense of humor. He remembered Sheila hadn't enjoyed his sense of humor. Neither had his last live-in, Melanie. She had been his first experiment with the pile of dirt. So far, so good.

Cherie moved quietly around the side of the house, dropping her stash of ammunition as she did. She was going to play by Jeff's rules; anything goes. She knew Jeff would go into the kitchen and expect to find her there. She had to hurry. She raced to the front of the house, picking up several cans of ravioli off the ground in front of the porch. She waited, crouched beside the porch steps until she heard him slam the kitchen door open. He should be finding the eggs she had thrown on the floor. She hurried to the front door and paused.

Jeff swung the kitchen door open with enough force to make it slam against the kitchen counter directly behind it. No Cherie. Where the hell did she go? She was acting strange today. It really pissed him off. She was going to pay for this. He strode through the kitchen toward the back door and stopped. Damn, his socks were wet from some sticky shit on the floor. He tore them off and charged through the back door and down the steps. He was going to kill her when he got his hands on her. Today.

Cherie heard the back door slam and ran back into the house directly up the stairs.

Jeff came around the side of the house just in time to see the front screen door close. What the hell kind of game was she playing? He started to run, nearly falling when his bare feet came down on Cherie's stash of beer bottle tops. Where in the hell had these come from? They were scattered everywhere! Damn!! He tore up the porch stairs into the house, intent on catching Cherie. When he got to the bottom of the stairs, he stopped to catch his breath and think. He stood bent over, hands on his knees, gasping from the exertion and the bottlecap cuts on his feet. The first can hit him square in the middle of his back, causing him to straighten and catch the next flying can in his shoulder.

"Damn, Cherie, what the hell are you doing? Trying to kill me?"

He looked up just in time to deflect the last can from hitting his head. The sonofabitches hurt!

"Do you feel more like Moe or Curly?" she said, standing at the top of the stairs, grinning at him. Jeff could not believe what he was seeing. She had gone insane.

"What the hell do you think you are doing?" He started up the stairs and abruptly stopped. Cherie raised a rifle, *his* rifle, and aimed it directly at him.

"Stop or I shoot your stupid, cowardly balls off, you shithead." Cherie had never felt so good her entire life as she did right now. He wouldn't threaten her and Jenny anymore.

Jeff grinned at her from the bottom of the stairs.

"You gotta be better than that to mess with old Jeff. You know I always win." He started up the stairs at her, and she cocked the rifle, pushing a bullet into the chamber. She smiled back and used her sweetest voice.

"Did I ever tell you how Daddy used to take me varmint hunting? He said I was the best little squirrel hunter in Cook County. Never missed a shot. How about you, shithead? Ever miss a shot?"

Cherie smiled again and pointed the muzzle of the rifle right at Jeff's crotch. She felt strong.

"You better quit screwing around with that gun. You're going to get someone hurt." Jeff wasn't sure if she knew the safety was on, or if she even knew about it. He figured he could take her in two steps. Rush her and maybe shake her up enough to make her drop it. She was going to pay for this.

Cherie knew Jeff would misjudge her. She also knew getting rid of him wouldn't be easy. She'd stopped in town after grocery shopping to call her ma and asked her to pick up Jenny from her friend's house and keep her for the night.

She had also talked to her old high school friend, a clerk in the sheriff 's office. After Cherie explained about Jeff's cruel behavior, her friend had run a check on him with several different police agencies. He was wanted in Michigan for questioning in the disappearance of a woman he had lived with. Ohio State Police were looking for him, too. He hadn't been a good boy in that state either. Cherie's friend had urged her to wait for the sheriff, but Cherie had some evening-up to do.

Driving home, she had planned different scenarios for getting to Jeff's gun before he did. He had played right into her hands.

"Come on, Cherie. You know you can't shoot me. I

won't hurt you. I promise."

Jeff smiled his best smile at her and took another step forward.

"Liar. You want to kill me right now. I'm tired of your shit and we are done. You are moving out today, this minute."

As Cherie clicked the safety off, Jeff made his move, taking two stairs at a time. She fired, the bullet tearing a hole in the top of his thigh; blood began pouring out. The force sent him back down the two steps he had taken toward Cherie. She cocked the rifle again, ready to shoot. He looked slowly up to Cherie, his face drained of color.

"I cannot believe you shot me with my own gun!"
He leaned against the wall next to the stairs, staring back down at his leg in disbelief.

The sound of tires on the driveway gravel distracted Cherie for a moment. Lunging up the stairs like a monkey, using his hands and feet for momentum, Jeff leapt at her. Cherie pulled the trigger at the same time as Jeff grabbed the end of the rifle. The bullet tore through his hand and sent him down the stairs, backwards. His head cracked against the railing and he tumbled limply the rest of the way down. He landed at the bottom, bleeding and unconscious as the sheriff burst through the screen door, gun in hand. Cherie lay the gun on the floor and sat down on the top step. No doubt about it, she could shoot a varmint dead on.

It was a fine day for varmint hunting.

Her daddy had never been wrong.

Juan Tesoro

John Deckinga

In the small village of Huixtla, far beyond the last town on the dusty road from the capital city of Durango, lived a magical boy named Juan Tesoro. What made him magical was that his body consisted of living crystal. He could walk and run and talk and laugh just like you and me, but, as you can imagine, he looked very different, like something from a story book.

> **John Deckinga**, originally from Chicago, lived for nearly fourteen years in Bolivia and Mexico. The strong influence of Latin American can be seen in much of his writing including this short story, *Juan Tesoro*. John currently does his writing in northern Michigan.

Juan had not always been magical. He used to be just like everyone else. But one day as he was tending his Uncle Lalo's sheep up in the mountains, he saw an angel. He has told us this, and we have no reason to doubt his word, although no one was with him at the time. We can certainly see that he is different now.

But this is how he tells it.

The angel appeared to him as he was resting during the noon hour. The angel did not speak directly to him, but instead began to sing a very beautiful song, so beautiful that Juan sat on the ground and wept for a long time with his head bowed. It was a song that made him very sad and very happy at the same time.

When the angel had finished, he came to where Juan was sitting and put his hand on Juan's shoulder. "Do you want to sing this song, Juan?" the angel asked him.

45

Juan nodded solemnly without looking up at the heavenly creature, then said softly, "Please, teach it to me."

So the angel taught Juan the song, and when he came back to our village in the evening, it was plain to see that he was different. He himself did not realize the change until someone called out to the others of the village, "Look at Juan!"

The whole village came and stared at Juan. It is hard to describe how he looked. I can only say it was something like living crystal. It was not that you could see the insides of Juan; it was more like you could see through him. But if you looked closer, you saw a red glowing thing, like a ruby, where his heart would be. Not a cold sparkling light, but rather a warm glowing, like the embers of a cooking fire.

After that, the life of the village changed very much, as you can well imagine. But it did not change all at once.

Juan continued to care for his Uncle Lalo's sheep. Every day he took them to the high pasture to feed and then herded them back down the mountain in the evening. When they were safely in the sheepfold, Juan made his way to the small village square where many of the townspeople met in the cool of the evening to talk and to listen.

The people of Huixtla are not impatient. They knew an amazing thing had happened to Juan, a miracle even. They did not ask to know everything all at once. This does not mean they were indifferent. On the contrary, they were very interested in knowing all about this extraordinary event. But they were willing to find things out slowly and to savor the finding out and the knowing.

At the village square one evening soon after Juan's amazing experience, Don Julio, the village cobbler and the oldest man in the village, a man very respected by all, asked Juan to tell them what had happened on the mountain.

"But please, Juan," he said, "take your time and tell us all the details you can remember."

Juan, in his quiet boy's voice, did so. He told of meeting the angel and of the song the angel had taught him. Slowly and clearly, he told what had happened. Then, unlike in the city where people are pushy and loud and ill-mannered, there was silence.

After a long while, some people began to talk quietly in little groups, confirming to each other the details of Juan's account and also exclaiming on the wonder of the experience. Then the people of the village went to their homes thinking about what they had heard.

The next several nights in the village square, first the old men, then most of the other adults and some of the children, asked Juan questions about what had happened, about things he hadn't mentioned the first time he told his story. How tall was the angel? What clothes did he wear? Did he offer Juan anything to eat? What did his voice sound like? What did he say exactly? Did he have a message for the people of Huixtla?

Juan answered each question. And each night the people of the village went home thinking about what Juan had told them.

Then, one evening, an evening everyone will always remember, one of the older women, Señora Castillo, the tortilla maker, asked Juan to sing the song the angel had taught him. Juan was not one of those people who like to be the center of attention. He was a simple shepherd boy. But he knew the song was important, for himself and for the people of Huixtla.

So he sang the song in a quiet voice. The sound of his voice was pure and clear, like water flowing over rocks in a mountain stream, like the notes of a flute played in the stillness of the evening. The music of it floated over the village square. Everyone was still and leaned forward to hear the song, even the little children and babies.

The effect of the song on the people was like what Juan had experienced with the angel--a mysterious mixture of sadness and happiness. It made the people look deeply inward, and when Juan finished no one spoke.

Finally, Don Julio, the same old man who had asked Juan to tell about his experience on the first evening, got stiffly to his feet, as old men do, smiled at Juan and shuffled home. Without a word others rose and also left, until the square was empty. Then Juan and his Uncle Lalo went home, too.

The next several evenings Juan was asked to sing his song again. Then Don Julio, who was really the leader of the village, looked at Juan and asked in a quiet voice, "Do you think it would be all right if we learned to sing the song, too? Did the angel say anything about that?"

"I think it is what he wants you to do," Juan answered simply. "I will teach it to you."

So Juan taught the song to the villagers. Some learned it quickly, and others took longer. A few people did not like the song and refused to learn it. These people usually stayed on the edge of the circle of villagers and simply watched or even scowled.

The effect of this whole experience--of Juan meeting the angel and learning the song and teaching it to the people of Huixtla--was not as immediately spectacular as one might think. I, for one, imagined that since this was supposed to be a miraculous event, the result of such an event should be that people would be healed from illnesses or even raised from the dead. But those things did not happen in our village.

What did happen was that the song made people

content, more aware of their lives and more able to bear their sufferings and their hard times. It also deepened the happy experiences of their lives.

The change was slow, but it was profound and affected many of the villagers. Not everyone, but the majority, yes.

Another important thing was that all this attention did not change Juan. He stayed the same, simple shepherd boy everyone had always known. He did not start a circus. He did not claim that the song was his property and charge people money to learn it. And he did not become a powerful politician or a great religious leader and try to sway people to his way of thinking.

He continued to tend his uncle's sheep, and he continued to be a shy, quiet boy. He was happy that the song was having such a good effect on the village, but he did not take credit for the change.

One day, however, he learned a frightening lesson. He was up in the mountains watching the sheep, as usual, when two boys stepped out from behind a tree where they had been hiding. They were the sons of two of the families who refused to learn the song. And even though they could clearly see that Juan had been changed into living crystal and that the song was having a good effect on the people of the village, in spite of these things, they started to chant at Juan, "The song's no good; you made it up. The song's no good; you made it up."

Juan tried to move his sheep away to another place, but the boys walked along, keeping pace with him and mocking him with their chant, "The song's no good; you made it up. The song's no good; you made it up."

Juan knew the boys were wrong. He knew he had seen an angel and had learned a beautiful song. And he knew he shouldn't get angry at them.

But he did get angry. And the more they chanted, the angrier he got. And this taunting did not happen only one time. Every day the boys followed Juan as he tended his uncle's sheep. And every day they chanted, "The song's no good; you made it up," at him. And Juan kept getting angrier.

One day as the boys chanted at him, Juan tried to sing the song he had learned from the angel, to take his mind off of their mocking. But he could not do it. And this, too, made him angry.

He tried again to sing the beautiful song, but the taunting of the boys and his own anger blocked it out. He could not sing the song.

Suddenly, Juan reached down and picked up a jagged black stone from the stream bed at his feet. Then he picked up another one. He stood up straight. The boys kept chanting, "The song's no good; you made it up."

Juan took the first stone and hurled it at the closest boy. It flew wide of the target. He hurled the second stone at the other boy, but it, too, missed its mark.

The two boys, seeing they had been successful in making Juan react in anger, laughed loudly and pointed at him. Then they turned and ran back down the mountain.

But the effect of his outburst was devastating on Juan himself. The blackness of his anger seethed inside him. He grew faint. He looked down and saw that the crystal of his body had become dull and the light of the ruby-glow had dimmed. He slumped to the ground unconscious.

When Juan did not return at the usual hour, his Uncle Lalo was not concerned at first. But when darkness fell and Juan had still not come back with the sheep, Uncle Lalo called a neighbor and they went up the mountain with lanterns and machetes, for there were still mountain lions in the area.

They found Juan, lying unconscious where he had fallen. They also saw that the ruby-glow of his heart, which they had become accustomed to seeing and which brought them great joy, was very dim. They knew something dreadful had happened.

Carefully they carried Juan down the mountain. The neighbor then went back to get the sheep for Uncle Lalo, while Uncle Lalo put Juan to bed. He had not regained consciousness.

The next morning there was no change in the boy. He lay pale on his bed, barely breathing. His poor uncle didn't know what to do. There was no doctor in Huixtla. But word of Juan's condition quickly spread through the village, and shortly after sunset that evening, Uncle Lalo heard a soft knock at the door.

It was Don Julio, the leader of the village. Uncle Lalo asked him to come in. In the dim light of the late evening, Uncle Lalo could see that there were many other villagers standing outside the door. Some held old lanterns. Others carried torches. They all stood quietly, not saying a word, concern written on their simple faces.

Don Julio took off his wide hat when he entered the house of Uncle Lalo, and without saying a word Uncle Lalo showed him to Juan's room. The old man sat down on a chair Uncle Lalo gave him. Don Julio could see that Juan was gravely ill, and the creases of his weathered face deepened when he saw the dullness of the ruby-glow. It was clear that Juan was dying.

Uncle Lalo stood by the door of the bedroom. Don Julio sat by the bed. The flame of the candle on the table in the corner hissed and flickered.

Several minutes passed and neither man spoke a word.

51

But the same question was tormenting them both. How could this young boy be dying? How could a miracle die? No answer came to them.

More silent minutes passed.

Then Don Julio straightened himself up and very softly, in a shaky old man's voice, he began to sing the special song this young boy had brought to their village. This was a moment of suffering and of pain, a good time to sing such a song.

The old man's scratchy voice could barely be heard, but as he continued to sing, his voice grew stronger. Some of the people outside the house heard snatches of the song, and soon they caught the rhythm and the words and began to sing along with the old man.

The song grew stronger and stronger as one by one the people outside took up the song. When they had finished, they began the song again.

In the room the two old men could see that the song was penetrating Juan's unconsciousness. Juan's brow began to furrow. His face twisted horribly, then smoothed; twisted again, then smoothed. Finally, the boy's face stayed smooth and still.

After several minutes he slowly opened his eyes. Don Julio smiled at him. But Juan did not smile back. Instead, in a very weak but urgent voice he rasped, "Tell Pepe and Beto to come." Then he lay quietly and closed his eyes.

It seemed like a very long time, but finally the two boys who had taunted Juan were found and brought to the house. They were shown into the bedroom, but stood just inside the curtained doorway. They shifted from one foot to the other, ill at ease, not sure why Juan had called for them, but ready to defend themselves.

Juan opened his eyes and looked directly at them. He

52

spoke very faintly, but they heard his words clearly in the quietness of the room. "I'm sorry that I got angry at you. It was wrong for me to throw those stones."

He said no more, simply closed his eyes again. The boys stood there for several minutes, still nervous, then they turned and went out of the house.

But Don Julio and Uncle Lalo, who were watching Juan very intently, saw a slow change take place in the young boy. They saw the ruby-glow grow ever so slightly stronger. Then stronger still. In a few minutes it was as strong and warm as before.

Juan opened his eyes and smiled at Don Julio and at his uncle. "Thank you," he said to Don Julio. And then he looked questioningly at his uncle. "The sheep?"

"They are all fine, Juan. Don't worry. I am happy you are better. Do you feel like eating anything?"

Juan nodded.

And in that tiny village of Huixtla at the foot of the high mountains far from the big city, the daily routine and rhythm of the village continued, but in its new way. As I said, it wasn't that there was no more pain, or sickness; there were still problems. It was just that in their everyday lives the people of the village acted differently.

And several weeks later Beto, one of the two boys, came to Juan while Juan was in the mountains tending his uncle's sheep. He asked Juan to teach him the song.

And Juan gladly taught it to me.

Voices of Michigan

The Gift

Kim Sanwald-Reimanis

Carl Kraus rose after a fitful night's sleep, strode over to the Venetian blinds on the window and peered out.

"Damn her!"

His eyes surveyed the damage. A large limb lay grasping tufts of his beautiful lawn with its fingers. He had told her six months ago to have that dead tree taken down. Now it was down, and he'd have to clean up the mess. He stalked off to his garden shed. There were limbs to dismantle, wood to be stacked, wounded areas to be raked and seeded.

For fifteen years, he had offered her sound, practical advice about preventing such episodes, yet she never seemed to take him seriously. Not much seemed to bother her, he thought, cleaning his safety glasses and placing them securely on his face. Being a pragmatic man, he had long ago eliminated all trees, shrubs and flowers from his property, opting for an undisrupted view of a lawn resembling a putting green. He primed his chain saw, set his jaw, and pulled. It coughed back. Carl pulled again. It roared to life. He deftly sliced through each limb, bringing order to the chaos.

> The creative process continues to mystify me. Writing brings me back to myself. It is the perpetual homecoming. To create, to allow a seed of thought to take root within me is deeply satisfying. I write for the sheer pleasure of it. I write because I must.

55

Carefully, neatly, he loaded wood into his wheelbarrow, then suddenly stopped and rubbed the stubble on his chin.

He didn't have a fireplace. She did.

Mumbling, he grabbed the wheelbarrow and pushed its wares into her driveway. The ruts vibrated his body. He quickly dodged the plastic gypsy lights she had strung haphazardly in the trees at eye level. Sometimes he spotted her at night, sitting in a lawn chair, regardless of the time or weather. He thought her a little balmy. She wouldn't mow, wouldn't repair, fill in, paint, or clean up. He shook his head and knocked briskly on the door.

"Come in, come in. I've just pulled scones from the oven."

The scent of baking held him for a moment. He blinked to break the spell.

"Can't stay, Miss O'Brien."

"All business? I bet you haven't even had your morning coffee."

Carl's stomach growled. "Thought you could use the wood."

Kate smiled warmly. "How kind of you, Carl; thanks so much. Grand storm, wasn't it? Reminded me of days on the Irish coast. Da and I would go up to Malin Head to watch horizontal rain."

Carl noticed the table meticulously set. "Expecting company?"

"Knew you'd be hungry. You were up and about so early." Kate's eyes held him.

"You know the rest of the tree has to come down."

"And disappoint my flickers and ladderbacks? Nature wastes nothing Carl."

Carl felt his left eye twitch. "Thanks for your offer; I'll take a rain check." He left abruptly and marched down the driveway.

Summer arrived with its cyclical frustrations. Carl poured boiling water into his mug of instant coffee and glanced at the window thermometer. Nine o'clock and already 70 degrees. Without hesitation, he grabbed his trowel from the garage and went out to do battle with the dandelions.

He heard humming next door and noticed Kate busy filling her feeders. He contemplated her investment in seed and imagined her going broke. At the boundary of their yards, he fell to his knees, his mood dark. He began digging, feverishly.

"Good morning, Carl."

"Just leave the 'good' off it."

"They'll come right back. Dandelions love the sun."

"Weeds are weeds."

"Weeds, like people, thrive when conditions are favorable."

"My grass would thrive if it wasn't competing for space."

Carl plunged his trowel into the soil. Of all the people to have as a neighbor, he thought. Her yard was a wilderness with its bird feeders and sprouting lawn. By the end of summer she would have to bale rather than mow. He noticed the ragweed and chicory were returning in profusion. Sweat rolled down his face as he carefully exorcised each weed. He found himself humming along with her. Few things brought him more pleasure than a lush, manicured lawn. It made him feel so civilized.

October brought clear skies and crisp weather. Carl stood tapping his head several times with the handle of his rake, lost in thought. Gusts of wind sent leaves swirling around him from neighboring yards. He knew most of them were Kate's. The crystalline fall day held no pleasure for him as he filled bag after bag and lined them neatly along the curb. Recognizing the sound of Kate's car he watched her pull into her driveway, get out, and stride briskly over.

"Just picked today. They're absolutely perfect!" Kate thrust a bag of Macintosh apples into Carl's arms. "I'll be baking a pie. Should I call you when it's ready?"

"No, thanks, need to finish this raking."

Kate stood munching an apple, the breeze blowing her hair in all directions. She resembled her yard, all colorful and untamed.

"Ever notice even the leaves in fields disappear by spring?"

Carl bit into an apple. The juice filled his mouth and oozed out the corner. He dropped his rake. Kate touched his forearm. The warmth of her fingers seared his skin and he stood outside himself as if looking through a camera lens, the aperture stopped down to control the light.

"Don't hesitate to change your mind."

Watching her walk energetically back to her car, he envied her enthusiasm, wished he knew how to accept her breezy invitation. He began wondering if he had been alone too long, dismissed the idea, and went back to his raking.

When a foot of snow fell just before Christmas, a hush settled over the neighborhood. Carl surveyed his newly shoveled driveway. He liked the contrast of the black top against the snow. Even Kate's yard looked clean and pristine.

Carl went inside, poured himself a small snifter of cognac, and sat down. Closing his eyes, he drifted until he thought he heard sleigh bells. A moment later, he heard them again. Opening his front door, he saw Kate, basket in hand.

"Merry Christmas, Carl. May I come in?"

There was a moment's hesitation. "Of course."

"I made this up especially for you. Fresh scones and a pound of coffee, plus a little something extra."

Carl lifted the treasures out of her basket, noting the scones were still warm. Beneath the delicacies, he saw a small feeder and a bag of birdseed.

"I don't know what to say."

"Then don't say anything."

"Excuse me just a moment."

Carl disappeared down the hall. He scanned his library, looking for something suitable for her. He suddenly found it. Important to strike just the right chord.

In his absence Kate noticed rows and rows of book shelves, the comfortable worn reading chair and the half empty glass. She took in the way the light cast warm shadows and knew Carl had depths well hidden from view.

Carl returned and handed Kate a book of cottage

gardens. He watched her eyes widen, and then she held the book against her.

"My mother had gardens very similar to these, Carl. They were absolutely beautiful, a riot of color. I remember her dreaming and plotting over seed catalogs. She had a knack for putting the most unusual combinations together with total confidence."

A cloak of awkwardness surrounded them. The hall clock chimed a warning, breaking the silence. Carl carefully folded himself up, like an unread letter.

"Sorry you can't stay longer Kate, but I wasn't expecting company."

"No problem, Carl; don't let me interrupt." Kate opened the door and slipped into the snowy night.

Several minutes passed before Carl noticed Kate had not moved from her position in front of the house. He opened his door.

"Are you all right?"

Kate turned toward him. The snow in her hair and the flush of her cheeks made her look like the very spirit of winter.

"Oh, Carl, the night is so delicious I could just cry with gratitude. Wouldn't you like to enjoy this?"

"I'm glad you're all right. Goodnight Kate."

Carl softly closed the door and leaned against it. He had never felt more alone. The loneliness increased later that evening when he looked out and saw Kate sitting under the gypsy lights, the snow falling softly around her.

Winter passed quietly for Carl. When spring came, he accepted an invitation to his brother's retirement dinner. He would be gone several days.

During his absence, the weather was unseasonably warm. Arriving home late, his headlights skimmed the front yard. He made a mental note to mow first thing tomorrow. It would feel good to return to his normal routine.

The next morning, he dressed quickly. His lawn beckoned. Peeking out his Venetian blinds, the brightness of the sun caught him off guard. Rubbing his eyes, he looked again.

"Damn her," he whispered. "Damn her," he smiled.

Along the length and breadth of his entire lawn were hundreds of blooming crocus.

Voices of Michigan

The Rare Book

R. C. Rutherford

I'd convinced myself many times: I thought I knew Emily Goodhart. She had worked in my rare book shop one year, ten months and three and a half days as my employee. My customers seemed to like Emily. Treated her as a normal, upstanding person. Emily developed our Internet catalogue. She acted intelligent. On time five days a week. The only abnormal thing about her, I thought lately, seemed to be a fascination with finding her mother. Then, disruption occurred last Thursday; Emily Goodhart disappeared. Now, on the following Monday, I look back on the last day I saw my employee. I don't have to tell you, people come and go, as especially employees will. Unfortunately, I had to ask myself why a priceless, signed, first edition of Ernest Hemingway's **The Old Man and the Sea** vanished the same time as my employee, Emily Goodhart.

R. C. Rutherford insists on letting his work speak for him. He isn't real certain why he writes, but he does enjoy a good story so tries to write good ones. He has always been in awe of what simple language can accom-plish. States Ruther-ford, "Books are a life in themselves, and I have kept myself under the illusion that I too have something to say."

I remember our last conversation. A cold spring day. My employee had burst into the store like a gust of last winter's air. Mrs. Peesky, one of our local customers, had been perched against the counter as she watched Emily crossing through the park. Mrs. Peesky said, "Here comes Emily. She's such a radiant girl. Do you know what I mean, Mr. Holbrook? You're lucky to have her here." I sorted through a recent collection of Robert Frost's original journals. I heard Mrs. Peesky, her voice a scratch on metal in the back of my head, my mind occupied with the work.

"Emily helps me decide on your lovely books, Mr. Holbrook. She should have a husband, though. Don't you think? Who knows in this day and age? She's really very good looking. Some young local could make a nice catch with her. All that long brown hair. Classical features. So right for our little Lake Michigan town. Don't you think, Mr. Holbrook?"

After Mrs. Peesky greeted my employee and left the store, my last conversation with Emily began. "You're late. First time ever, Ms. Goodhart," I said. My employee appeared distracted. A misplaced conception in her twenty-eight year old eyes, face transformed. Taut with a muscle contraction, a flash of a shaded gray shadow across pearl white flesh, a mask I had never witnessed. This odd behavior must be a result of her recent obsession to locate her mother. I remember the walnut trees in the park in front, forcing their foliage on the season, the mowed grass weeks ahead of the walnut trees when it came time to regroup after an arduous Michigan winter. Emily brushed past me like wind-blown newspaper, heading to her computer room. I followed.

She spoke as she sat down at her desk: "Sorry, Arthur, I should have called. I've had this work at home. I hoped you wouldn't mind. Did you see the message from Seattle I left last night?

"Yes, I saw the pad of paper. Did you tell the guy none

of those books were for sale?"

"Of course, I've heard you turn down a hundred offers. Nothing's for sale out of the special case." The bell on the front door sounded and I went out front to mind the store. Mrs. Brimley, who owned the antique store next to my book store, had sink problems again. I went to help and when I returned, I'm sure no less than a half hour later, my employee had disappeared. I found the lock on the special bookcase forced, the rare Hemingway missing.

I sat at the front counter of my book store three days later, expecting my employee to come quavering through the front door any minute. Of course, I doubt this now. Three days without a word. (I haven't reported her missing or the theft.) I still believe an explanation will surface, people's problems can transform into complications in our little Northern Michigan town. I've made up my mind, though, to look for her, talk to her landlord.

I closed the store and walked the three blocks to my employee's rooming house. She occupied a small apartment at the rear of the elegant looking Victorian house. A Mrs. Chance opened the door. Mrs. Chance's eyes seemed to hold some knowledge of the situation. Her eyelids fluttered like the wings of a butterfly. She said, "Mr. Holbrook, come in."

"You know me?"

"Of course. Emily adores you. She tells me all about you and the store. She loves your rare books, likes you and your wool suits. Stuff like that. Life in general in our little town. Emily and I are very good friends."

"She hasn't been to work in three days. She vanished when I stepped out of the shop. Have you seen her? She didn't answer my knock, doesn't answer her phone. What is it, Mrs. Chance? You look worried."

"You are right. She has disappeared. I had hoped she was staying elsewhere, but I guess she would have told me. Maybe it's a man she doesn't want me to know about. But missing work? That's not her way. Something must be wrong."

"Did she have a boy friend? Notice anything strange the last couple of months?"

"She's been trying to find her mother. You know Emily was a foster child from birth. Her mother gave her up then. Could she have located her and gone to her?"

"That's possible. She had spoken very little to me about it. Some Internet work. Did she have anybody close that you know of?"

"Go see Denise O'Mally. She lives in a blue house behind a cedar hedge. There's a giant pine growing close to the house, three blocks up on Beech street."

"If my employee calls or comes home, call me immediately. Thanks Mrs. Chance."

I walked up the hill where mature Maple trees lined the street, the street like an aisle of a church. The human face like facades of the old style houses had personalities. I knocked several times on the Beech street house. Shade from old Maple, leaning Cedar trees and a wide porch overhang darkened the front stoop. A door opened. A blond girl with hooded eyes stood behind the screen clutching a robe around herself. She squinted at the filtered sunlight, the house behind her dark. I said: "I'm Arthur Holbrook. Is Emily Goodhart here?"

"No."

"Do you have any idea where she might be?"

"Is she in some kind of trouble? You're her boss, right?"

"Yes. She works at my bookstore."

"She hasn't been by here in a week. You look like a lawyer in that suit."

"Did she mention any changes...or trips to you...in say...the last month? Maybe her lost mother?"

"Well, yeah. Emily became obsessed with the idea she had a real biological mother in the world. Emily had an institutionalized upbringing. She's too adult for her age. Those places made her grow up to early."

"She's looking for her lost youth. And I might be financing the trip. Can you keep a secret, Ms. O'Mally? You seem very intelligent. A very valuable book went missing around the time my employee did."

"How valuable?"

"Priceless to me. Fifty thousand on the market in a quick sale with no authorization of authenticity. I still have that. I'm not saying Emily stole the book. I was out of the store."

"I don't believe for one second my friend would take such a risk. She talks too much about how she likes working in your store. All those old books and stuff, the mysteries, working with the computer - all that, I can tell you was important to her."

"If you were thirty years old, trying to make life decisions, had no help from your parents and then found your real Mother, you might take a risk. I got the feeling she was embarrassed about her past. I wish she had said something to me. I could have helped."

"Well, if she did take off she had to travel... and not on foot. Call around to various travel services; I mean, find out if she left town."

I walked back down the hill, catching glimpses of the blue waters of the bay through rooftops and trees. A cool wind caressed the town. A police car drove down the street, and I wondered if I should go to the police. I wanted to protect my employee. Emily was innocent until proven guilty. In our small town, you were guilty until proven innocent. I had to think about why my employee might have lifted the Hemingway. Her mother could have been in some far-off, out-the-way spot. With my employee's ability with Internet search sites, I started thinking she might have found her mother and financed the trip with the sale of the Hemingway. Could she have sold it to the guy coming in from Seattle and scooted? She was alone in the shop for no more than a half hour. What the hell could have happened?

I went up the back way to my two story townhouse above the book shop. I looked out over the tops of several buildings across the flat shimmering waters of the bay. Still cool for May. I set some logs burning in the fireplace. Then, I sat down at the dinning room table with the local phone book, and I checked Pellston airport, the bus line, the taxicab service, and the car rentals. My employee wasn't traveling by these methods. A borrowed car?

A day and half later, after touring a three county range of small craft landing strips, I found a guy in Indian River who had flown a girl to a private landing strip in the Upper Peninsula to a farm with enough flat pasture to land a 747 near Dryburg. The pilot said she had left the same day my employee vacated my store. I asked, "Was she alone? Did she have luggage? Did she drive here?"

"Just a back-pack thing. Looked like she walked here. Said she had the summer off."

"What did the farm look like?"

"Run down. Kind of spooky. I got back across the straits on a bee line."

"Where was the farm in relation to the town."
"North. Couple of miles."

Next morning the steel grating on the Mackinac
Bridge roadway had my tires humming. At the top of the
suspension arch, I had to wonder, already an hour away from
home, what was I chasing? Of course the invaluable signed
Hemingway was first on my mind; the author had signed his
name and added the message: "Stay away from journalism,
Bob." Whoever Bob was. No rare book expert knew. Many
experts upon examining the book, wanted to buy it, but I
think I wanted to find my employee just as much as the book.
She had become, in this past year, like the daughter I never
had. I spoiled her, overpaid her, bought the expensive
computer. She had begun to pay her own way with the,
"Holbrook Rare Titles" web site. Is she really up at some old
farm in the U.P.? Why hadn't I intervened more in her recent
preoccupation? A long lost mother? In my mind I composed
the creed to all free youth: "Fly from the nest and do not
return."
        I crossed the "Mighty Mack" and cruised up I-75. The
car I drove had a knock in a cylinder. I thought the car might
burst its engine any second. I drove, clutched to the wheel
like it was a life vest and my trip an excursion into the worst
oceanic conditions. I found the old Swedish farm several
hours later. It belonged to Mr. August Crabtree. I sat in his
kitchen an hour before we realized we weren't talking about
the same girl. He had never heard of Emily Goodhart. I sat
and talked with the old guy for a while anyway. We drank
potent, homemade mash from his still. A large jet-black raven
perched on a twisted Cedar branch nailed to the wall and
squawked for attention. Mr. Crabtree wanted to know more

about this girl, my employee. His hootch and loneliness must have made the story interesting. I told him the story.

"Sounds like a nice lady and a hell of situation," Mr. Crabtree said.

"Yes. Emily's a fine young girl, really a woman. Girl doesn't fit. Except...she...I have to confess, I knew nothing of her background. She was my employee. I was hoping the girl the pilot dropped off in your field might have been her."

"No sir. I wish I coulda helped you out. That girl the plane dropped off is the neighbor girl up from college. Used my field. I wish you the best of luck. You sure you can drive?"

My head buzzed from the old guy's booze. I had drunk in celebration for being hot on my employee's tail. The alcohol diluted the fact that I had wasted my time on a wild goose chase.

One time Emily, she had just started as my employee, had an encounter with an obnoxious customer. I stood behind a bookcase and overheard my employee handle the situation:

"The price reflects the fact it is a rare item, sir. You might see it as an investment. And you get to enjoy the book for its story, sort of a perk from your investment." I had this memory of Emily as I drove back home. My employee had vanished. Who was there to really care? I certainly did. This was the fourth day. And then I realized I should have checked our computer. I called a friend, Dan Strange, who's a PC whiz kid and asked him to meet me at the book store in one hour.

"Know her password?" Dan asked.

"This is Emily's machine. I'm too old to learn computers," I said.

"All righty, then. Let's see what we come up with."

The whiz had the machine humming and whirring, and I saw our web site spread. Colors flashed.

"Anything?" I asked.

"Here's your incoming E-mail file. It wants a pass word. Any ideas? Something simple most likely. One word."

"She loves Hemingway. Try Pappa."

"Very good." I watched him type the name.

"Presto. We're in. Smart, Arthur."

"See if you can find any attempt at corresponding with a missing persons' bureau or something like that."

"Most of this looks like catalogue requests. Here's one labeled with the word 'lost'."

"Open it." I scanned the message E-mailed from an Internet company. They had found my employee's real mother. "They don't say where her mother is. Anything more?" I asked.

"OK. A little further. Here's some more stuff. Says this woman lives right here in Petoskey."

I collapsed on an authentic, sixteenth-century, Chinese, opium-smoking couch in Mrs. Brimley's furniture boutique. Mrs. Brimley poked a cup of coffee mixed with strange herbs at me. I stared at a dusty moose mount on the wall. I said: "Do you know this woman, Mrs. Brimley? My employee's real mother? This Rhonda Smith? Apparently she lives in a trailer out on Atkins Road."

"I haven't the foggiest idea. You have to go see her, Arthur. And you have to eat something. Get to the bottom of this before it drives you nuts. And think of the Hemingway book. It's worth a lot of money."

"My employee wouldn't just give this woman the book."

"The girl was looking for her real mother, Arthur. It

seems as though she found her. It's a step in finding this valuable object. Maybe Emily gave her the book for the money. Fifty-thousand is enough to take a chance."

"More valuable to me, Mrs. Brimley, than money. I'll go to the trailer on Atkins Road, and then I'll eat."

The trailer sat in a hardwood plot in a series of rolling meadows. The bright, spring-green colors spread across the landscape like a tapestry. A rangy hound met me on the two-track leading to the trailer. Was this where my employee's mother lived?   I passed several discarded old heap automobiles, exiled appliances, a large black iron kettle hanging from a sapling tree tripod, stacks of wood and some wire mesh bird pens. It wasn't a trailer my employee's mother lived in. This was a nineteen 'sixty-ish' Winnebago. A stout, red haired woman in men's clothes eyeballed me from a chicken-coop. A hound raced around my car. Rhonda Smith did not look happy to see a stranger. I rolled down the window of my car. Rhonda clenched a rake in her brown hands. The dog raised up on the car door.

"Brubaker, get over here," she yelled. The dog obeyed her. She leaned against the rake as I rolled out of the car. I said, "Rhonda Smith? I'm Emily Goodhart's employer."

"I don't think you should be here, Mr. Holbrook. Emily and I have it worked out."

"Where the hell is she?"

Rhonda looked away and began to rake up dirt. "You're gonna get your shoes dirty, Mr. Holbrook, better just head back to town." A Mourning Dove tried to land on my shoulder. Shafts of spring sunlight filtered down through the trees, shimmering off leaves and branches. I could smell the Winnebago's sewage. Rhonda Smith walked away. I couldn't mention the book. I had to find unmistakable proof of what happened.

I returned home, unhappy and had a restless night.

...I'm frustrated...angry...my hands feel like boat paddles...I can't keep the water out of this meager one man skiff...all I can see is green water...Lake Michigan? I look up at the sky and it's a rolling mass of pewter-gray clouds...instantly the cloud mass opens to reveal a full moon. This moon is my prey...it is my job to kill the moon. I try to row the skiff towards the globe...floating on top of the orb's molten water reflection...I'm armed with only a fishing pole, and I must kill the moon? Why not the sun also? And the stars? I couldn't kill the moon, the sun or the stars in ten life times...I feel uncomfortable...I hate a job you could never accomplish.... I try for a day and a half to forget this dream. We are born lucky, not to have to kill these monsters, I thought.

The next day, I decided it was time to notify the police.

Detective Dunston Dupree, of the Petoskey police department wanted to talk first edition books. I'd known him since he ran the streets as a kid in Petoskey, thirty-five years ago. I sat at a chair opposite his desk at police headquarters on the waterfront where the Bear River empties into Little Traverse Bay. Dun has jet-black hair he combs back on his head like a helmet. He wears blue jeans and Hawaiian shirts, cowboy boots. He said: "You should have come to see me earlier, Arthur. We've had trouble with rip-offs downtown. Someone is sneaking around back alleys and shoplifting in broad day light. This perp coulda' lifted your Hemingway."

"What about my employee?"

"I know all about Emily and her mother, Rhonda Smith, and her story. Emily probably got tired of our small town. Rhonda's not what you call a great surprise Mother. Remember, I'm a regular customer of your bookstore. If you didn't spend so much time in Mrs. Brimely's antique shop, you might know more about what's going on Arthur."

"I haven't seen you around for weeks and you tell me you know what's going on. Emily is missing, Detective. And so is my book." He lifted his boots off his desk, drew his fingers through his black helmet of hair, adjusted his bright colored shirt. Dunn's phone started ringing. He looked at me with a furrowed brow, tapped a pencil on his desk. He turned his back on me, answered the phone and held a whispered conversation. Ten minutes later, we were driving north out of town in the detective's undercover car headed for a deserted stretch of Lake Michigan beach.

"I can't believe this story you're trying to put over on me," I said to the detective.

"I didn't make the call, Arthur."

"My employee, missing almost a week, has been held hostage all this time at a beach house on Sturgeon Bay?"

"I guess she slipped away to a house down the beach. These places are spread apart. She's at this neighbor's house now. That was what the call was about. Some old man lives there. He called it in to the sheriff. Sheriff called me. This is your Emily. Got in the middle of a robbery or something. She's hurt and incoherent. She told the old guy she didn't think the kidnapper knew she was gone yet. The sheriff has the kidnapper's beach house blocked off."

"This is absurd. Kidnapped? I thought my employee had found her long lost mother and donated the missing book to her so my employee's mother could do something about her living situation. All along, I guess I thought my employee was a thief."

"You should be more trusting, Arthur."

We drove through the Bliss swamp. Lake Michigan came into view over the tree line. The lake a wide plane of dark blue out to the horizon. Beach grass dotted the buff colored sand. Dunn and I pulled up to a shingle-sided cottage. I didn't see another house. I said, "There she is on the deck."

"Hey, look, let me handle this," Dunn said. Nonetheless, I rolled out of the car and headed straight to my employee. Emily lay on a deck lounger wrapped in a large blanket. She had a vacant look as she stared out across Lake Michigan.

"Emily. Are you all right?" I asked. I could tell she had been slapped in the face. Both eyes were ringed with yellow, black, and cobalt. She had an open cut on her lip. "She's had the shit kicked out of her Detective. What the hell happened, Emily?"

"He wanted the book, Arthur." She looked away from me.

"We got him, Emily. You're OK now. Tell us what happened," Dunn said.

"I don't think now's the time...," I began.

"It's all right, Arthur. I saved the book. I've got it right here. The bastard picked the lock in the special cabinet. He asked me to get something from the computer. I saw him leaving, and I followed him to his rental car. It's that guy from Seattle. He was obsessed with this book. When he saw me following after him, I walked up to him and demanded the Hemingway back. He pulled my arm behind my back and forced me into his car. I ended up in that desolate place, locked in a closet for days; I could hear the waves hitting the beach, and the bastard using the phone to some sheik who was going to land a seaplane and buy the Hemingway for one-

75

million dollars. He'd open up the door and kick me; said I was the reason the deal had gone wrong for him. I jimmied the door when I thought he was sleeping. The Hemingway was right there on the table, so I just grabbed it and left."

"You walked to this place?" Dunn asked.

"I was on the beach for a while, I think, then the road. It was pitch black; I was scared out of my mind. I felt like a little lost girl, stumbling along. I kept thinking of those cheap horror movies or those thriller books, like I was just acting through this character who wasn't really me. I didn't know where I was or what day or night it was. I remember trying to keep the happy idea in my mind that I had found my real mother, and I had the book. Arthur, I was so tired. I was thinking of you. I knew I didn't want to be locked up in that closet again where that creep could do anything he wanted to me. I'd like to be able to shoot him if I see him, Dunn. Can I shoot him, Dunn? We're a still a team, aren't we, Arthur?"

"Of course. You're my employee, Ms. Goodhart." That's all I could think of to say to her.

"EMT is here." Dunn said. My employee had fallen asleep.

Midlife Crisis

Mary Lee Scott

Her 35th birthday began like any other day. The radio alarm played a song from 1981, her senior year in high school. (She kept all radios tuned to "oldies.") She shut off John Cougar (Not yet Mellencamp), then lay back reflecting on the dream she'd had, about Brett Favre. She had always been interested in dreams. This one would be fun to share with Mike. Of course, some dreams were taboo to discuss, even with the one you shared your life with, but most he enjoyed hearing and teased her about. She realized that he never confessed to dreaming about another woman. She didn't press this issue. It was probably just as well.

Mary Lee Scott is a 36-year old elementary school teacher who lives with her husband and two sons, ages 8 and 11, in Galesburg, Michigan. She loves reading and writing and recently won first-prize in the Kalamazoo Gazette's Community Literary Awards. Her life goal is to publish a novel.

She was about to get up and wake the boys when the phone rang. Her first thought was, "Mike's going to wish me Happy Birthday." He had left for work as a police officer an hour before she and the boys got up. "Hello?" she said, in a singsong voice. Instantly, she knew she was wrong. There was a brief pause, then, "Mary?" At first, she did not recognize the deep voice. "Yes," she answered tentatively. "It's Mark Johnson from the department," said the voice. In her mind she saw Johnson dressed up for a luau at her and Mike's house. Johnson had a sheet and flowered lei necklace, and carried a stick upon which a plastic shrunken head had been mounted. He was supposed to be "Big Chief Wiki-Wiki," and had played the part to the hilt, much to the delight of everyone, especially Evan and Sean, their sons.

She swallowed. "Hi, Mark," she said, trying to keep her tone light, hoping that she could change the direction in which she was sure this conversation was going. "Mary, I've got to tell you some bad news," he said, and she sat straight up. "What?" she cried, then remembered the sleeping children. She lowered her voice. "What's wrong, Mark?"

"It's Mike. He's been shot, Mary. He's at St. Joseph's now."

"Oh, God. How bad is it?" She waited, not breathing. Now she understood how hearts could skip a beat.

"He's alive, and Mary, I don't know how bad it is Everything around here is crazy. It happened as soon as he hit the street. Some idiot..." His voice broke. She could picture him in the radio room, trying to keep his composure.

"Mark, thanks for calling me. I have to go now," she said. Instantly she was on a high like caffeine, ready to do anything to get to St. Joseph's. She had an impulse to run there. She hung up the phone. Oddly, the first person she thought to call was her boss, the principal of Pine Forest Elementary School. She knew from years of teaching that finding a substitute teacher could be a time-consuming task.

What was she thinking? Had her dedication to her job made her a complete moron? Why was she worrying about her classroom when her husband had been shot?

She didn't have much experience in crises. Her

mother had always been calm, and had expected it in her children.. Nothing in this world was worth raising your voice over, or worse, crying about. She raced down the stairs to the den, where the phone numbers were kept.

She found her principal's number, then pushed the buttons on the den phone. It amazed her how smoothly her fingers worked, how quickly the connection was made. He answered on the third ring, sounding rushed. "Rob? It's Mary Walsh." As always, she waited for the other person to greet her. As he always did, he said nothing, just waited for her to explain why she was calling him at home at this hour. She couldn't believe how calm her voice was.

"I can't come in today. Mike's been shot. I have to go to the hospital." She stopped speaking and breathed the way they taught her when she and Mike had gone to Lamaze classes before Evan was born. She heard Rob say, "Mary, I'm so sorry. How badly is he hurt?"

"I don't know. I'm leaving right now. I'll call later and let you or Margie know." Margie, her best friend at school, taught second grade next door.

"Don't worry about anything. We'll get a sub in your room, and Mike'll be fine. Mary, he's young, he's strong..." He was saying all the right things.

She cut him off. "Thanks, Rob. I've got to go now." She didn't want to hear comforting words, just wanted to go. She had to get her parents to come sit with the boys; they couldn't go to school. She had to call Mike's parents.

She dialed her parents quickly, knowing her mother would answer the phone. When she did, Mary spoke briefly, telling her what had happened. "We'll be right there," her mother said, and almost as an afterthought, "He'll be all right,

Mare. He's a tough old bird." Her mother had said the same thing to her each time she called to say she was in labor. "You're a tough old bird." Where in hell did an expression like that come from? Were certain birds known to be tough? If so, which ones?

She wondered about that as she dialed her in-laws, knowing that this call would not be so easy. Making matters worse, Evan and Sean came pounding down the stairs, stopping before they got to her to stare. She covered the receiver with her left hand.

"Boys, go upstairs and get dressed. I'll tell you what's going on as soon as I call Grandma."

They answered her at the same time, Sean asking which grandma she was calling, Evan saying in a very frightened voice, "What's wrong?" Evan always thought the worst about a situation. This time he was accurate.

"I said go upstairs. I'll tell you in a minute." She glared at the boys, sending Sean scurrying for the stairs, but only making Evan's pale face look more pinched. "Mom..." he pleaded.

"Hello?" she heard her mother-in-law say, then realized she had said it at least once before. "Cindy?" she blurted before she remembered that her mother-in-law wanted her to call her Mom. It was certainly nothing personal--she loved Mike's mother like a dear friend--but she, nonetheless, could hardly bring herself to address her by this title.

"Mary? Is it you? What's wrong?" There was fear in her voice. She sounded as if she was already going to cry.

"It's me. It's bad news. Mike's been hurt."

She heard her mother-in-law inhale sharply. "What

happened?"

"He was shot. I don't know how bad he is. I'm going to St. Joseph's now. I'll meet you there," she said as quickly as she could, not wanting the conversation to drag out. She had to get to Mike.

Cindy didn't ask anything else. "I'll get Dad. We'll be right there. Mary, do you want to ride with us?"

"No, thanks. I want to go right now. I'll see you in a few minutes." She definitely did not want to wait or to be driven. She hung up the phone as she heard Cindy say, "Be careful. Try not to worry." She looked up from the phone. Ten-year-old Evan was standing before her, tears filling his eyes. She went to him and took him in her arms, not an easy task. Evan was almost as tall as she and weighed the same. These qualities were helping him in rocket football, but hindering him at the moment.

"Honey, he'll be OK. We just have to pray, and believe that he is so strong, he'll get through it." She sounded trite. Maybe he was too young to know cliches when he heard them.

He wasn't. "You don't even know how he is. I heard you telling Grandma. I'm going with you." His face was miserable, scared, and reproachful at the same time.

"Honey, listen to me." She was trying to be the role model all the articles said she should be. She must not fall apart and spill her fears onto him. "You can't go yet. As soon as I know anything, I promise I'll call you. You and Sean stay here with Grandma. You don't have to go to school today, so you can visit Daddy when the doctors say it's OK."

She was making this up, hoping that they would indeed be visiting their father that day. She had a fleeting

81

image of the boys walking into a hospital room, Mike lying on an adjustable bed with just a cast on his arm, laughing about not being able to throw the football to them for a while. "Please, God, let it be so mild," she thought.

And then she heard her parents pull into the driveway. She jumped up. She was running up the stairs as she pulled off her jersey, calling to the boys. "Evan, I need you to help Grandma. Be helpful, and be nice to Sean. He'll be worried. Sean, I'm going to see Daddy. He got hurt at work. He's at the hospital."

Sean bolted out of his room and asked, "Did he get shot?" She remembered that both boys had mentioned fearing this. She supposed it was the influence of TV or even things other kids said. Sean's brown eyes, so like hers, were huge. He hugged her as she was finishing dressing. She picked him up, and he held on.

"Honey, I have to go. Grandma is here. You don't even have to go to school today, so I can call you when I hear about Daddy." He brightened briefly at the news of being able to stay home from school, then sagged again.

She set him down next to Evan, who had wordlessly joined them. "Guys, I can't talk now because I don't know anything. I'll call you as soon as I can."

"Mom?" Evan looked at her. "Did they catch the person who shot Dad yet?"

"I don't know, but if they didn't, you can bet that there are many deputies looking right now." This time she knew she spoke the truth. There was no one more wanted by the police than one who hurt their own.

She ran down the stairs, knowing that she hadn't combed her hair or brushed her teeth. At the front door stood her parents. She was so glad to see them; now she could get to Mike. It seemed like hours since Mark's phone call. Her parents came in, murmuring comforting words. She grabbed her purse, hugged each son and was in the garage, starting the van. She saw her father approaching.

"Drive carefully," was all he said. He handed her a Diet Coke, caffeine-free. That was her preferred drink "I will," she answered, and backed out of the driveway very slowly. She drove by the house with the van's interior light on, waving. This was their tradition. Both boys and her mother waved back at her.

She gunned the accelerator as soon as she turned onto the busier road. Her mind raced...

She saw Mike at seventeen, picking her up and squeezing her after a big football victory... At twenty-three, smiling down at her and saying, "I will." They both had, for twelve years. Last night, they had made love. It had been so perfect, so pure, she had wanted to cry. Her insides tingled briefly. They knew how fortunate they were, she and Mike, had seen other couples their age unhappy.

Her age!! She was 35! How could it be, when she felt great and remembered everything? Only her hair had changed, a tiny bit of gray showing in the brown. Oh, and her face was beginning to develop lines around her eyes, from so much sunbathing (and smiling, she hoped). It really was true, what they said about years flying by.

More memories... Talking in bed far into the night... Watching the boys play baseball during the summer... Holding hands as they walked along their favorite northern Florida beach... Mike saying, "Marrying you was the best thing I ever did."

She paused at a stoplight and shook her head. She turned on the oldies station, loud. It was playing an REO Speedwagon song. They had seen REO in concert the summer before.

She was at St. Joseph's. She didn't recall getting there. Were guardian angels real? She drove right to the ER, where she saw several police cars. A deputy she didn't know met her at the van and said, "Mary? I'll take you in to him."

"How is he?" She didn't know if she wanted to hear. He opened the door for her, and they walked quickly down the white hall. The smells hit her - disinfectant, cafeteria food, cleaning supplies, and coffee - all at once.

"He's going to be all right, Mary," the young officer told her, smiling. "Here he is."

She hesitated; there were so many people standing around the bed, mostly doctors and nurses, but a few officers, too. They parted for her, and she saw Mike's best friend reach his hand out for her. Jim brought her to the bed where her husband lay, looking ashen. She approached, and suddenly didn't know what to say. He had an IV in one arm and was bandaged around his abdomen.

"Hey," he said softly when he felt her touch his hand.

She felt her knees giving out. She was so happy to see him conscious. She tried not to cry, but tears began to spill. Relief, mixed with worry, took over. One of the deputies brought a chair and eased her into it, where she put her face in her hands and cried.

"Mare, Mare, it's not bad," Mike said. He put his hand on her head, which couldn't have been easy considering the I.V. "I took one in the stomach, but the vest saved me. Just broke a couple of ribs. I think I'll make one of those commercials." He was referring to the commercials about the bulletproof vests, which she switched off every time they appeared on the TV screen. His voice sounded normal, quieter than usual.

She fished a tissue from her well-stocked purse and dried her face. She felt Jim's hand on her shoulder behind her. She smiled at Mike, then stood and leaned over him. She kissed him gently and whispered, "How do you feel? Does it hurt?"

He smiled at her without lifting his head. "Not much. All I could think of when I saw the gun was you and the kids. But it's over now. Soon I'll be vacuuming again." He always did that job; she detested it. He smiled. "Happy Birthday, Mary."

It would be her best.

Voices of Michigan

River Ghost

Charles Sams

I think I was born with a fly rod in my hand, but it was my love of stories that took time to develop. Fly fishing was a natural passion, and by the time I was eighteen, I could not recall the very first time I had cast a fly to a waiting trout. Fly fishing was also the reason, in the summer of 1955, that I learned to love stories. It was the trout that had brought the most famous fly fisherman to the river, and it was that fisherman who brought the wonder of imagination to me.

Charles Sams has lived in St. Clair Shores, Michigan for much of the last 13 years. He works as a Quality Engineer for a major automotive supplier, and has had thirteen short stories published in the **Woods-N-Water News.** The outdoor activities of Michigan play a large roll in Charles' writing as well as the influence of authors Tom Carney, Jerry Dennis, Harper Lee and John Steinbeck.

The first time I had heard of this man was in school, but I paid no attention to him. I did not care about stories; I only wanted to learn how to read, write, add, and subtract. These subjects coupled with a strong back were all that I would need to make it in the timber business. My life plan, at eighteen, was to work in my father's mill and spend my leisure time catching trout in the river and playing my music. That all changed, though, in late June that year when Ernest showed up and turned the town and my future upside down.

87

I remember the time of year well because in mid-to late June, the giant Mayflies hatch, Hexagenia Limbata or the "Hex" as it is known by the fly fisherman. Fishermen come from near and far to fish the Hex hatch as the flies entice the big Brown and Rainbow trout to the surface. There is a trick to fishing the Hex hatch; the flies hatch only during the black of night well after the witching hour. Fishing the Boardman at night, even with the aid of today's technology, is no easy task, much less trying to do it more than forty years ago when most of us in the north were still well behind the cities.   Fly fishing at night requires extensive daytime scouting and at least one person who knows the river like the back of his hand. I knew the river that well; it was literally my back yard. and most people in that area knew of my knack for being able to fish the Hex hatch successfully.

I had finished my work at the mill early, as I often did during the Hex hatch, and headed straight for the river to stake out a good stretch before dark. I fished the smaller trout while it was still light, making casts to likely holes and memorizing the snags and other obstacles. I was in the middle of making a roll cast up under some over-hanging branches when I heard footsteps behind me, at the edge of the river. I turned to see the figure of a man standing on the bank, outlined by the evening dew and the setting sun; he appeared as I imagined ghosts would.

"William?" A strong voice boomed from the bank.

"Who wants to know?" I answered with my own question.

The man entered the river, and as he came closer, I was able to start to make out some of his features. He was of average build, possibly even a little thick for his height.

He wore a wide brim hat, bigger than any that I had ever seen anyone wear on the river; it cast a dark shadow over his already tanned, weather-beaten face.   His upper lip carried a thick black mustache, which, coupled with the tan, gave the impression that he was of Latin or Spanish descent. He wore a pair of rubber chest waders tightened at the waist by a leather belt and carried what I immediately recognized as an L.L. Bean fly rod and reel in his left hand. I knew he could not be from within a hundred miles of the river; no fisherman that I knew could afford chest waders and an L.L. Bean rod. Even most of the visitors from down state, the people with good jobs in the auto factories, could not afford such luxuries. They normally just waded in an old pair of shoes and pants and fished with second hand rods as I did.

"The name is Ernest," the man said as he extended his right hand. "People in town said that I might find you here; I'm interested in fishing the Hex hatch; they said that you were the man to see. I'm willing to pay you for your services as a guide for the night."

I had never had anyone offer to pay me before; usually I just traded something like eggs, milk, or beer for a night's fishing. Thoughts of what I could do with cash sent my mind spinning, and I accepted the job as guide. I figured Ernest was just a green horn with too much money to spare; I took the job without giving it any real thought. I had no idea whom I was dealing with.

I explained to Ernest that I had fished this stretch of the river before and that I had scouted it earlier in the day, during my lunch break from the mill.

"This stretch holds good numbers of trout during the day and at night, during the hex hatch; I have taken

89

many large browns from here. We will do well," I told Ernest.

"Good, then let's get started," he said as he slowly clicked the line from his reel and cast to the last of the daytime trout. "It won't be long now."

Ernest's teeth gleamed white, in the dying purple light, as he flashed a big smile from underneath his mustache. He was standing to my sundown side, and the last of the soft light silhouetted his wide brimmed form, tickling his edges, again giving him a ghostly feel. Even as all light began to fade completely and Ernest lost his haunting glow, I could still feel his energy. Then, with just a sliver of light left in the day, he set the hook and a large trout exploded from the river as if shot from a cannon. The Hex hatch had not even started, and he already had on one of the largest trout that I had ever seen; I understood that he needed me only for my knowledge of the river's structure. I also knew that I was in for a special night of fly fishing. Little did I know that what I would learn that night would have an effect on the rest of my life. Ernest brought the big Brown to hand and released it back to the gripping fingers of the river's flow.

"Let's get ready for this hatch," Ernest said as he forced his body through the current back toward the bank. We sat on the bank, tied on or hex imitations, and discussed our strategy.

"It's a waiting game now; we wait for the hatch to fall, and then we listen for the slurping of the feeding trout. In the meantime, we light a fire and relax," I instructed.

Our gear in order, we leaned our rods against a tree, picking out the most conspicuous so as not to lose them in the dark. I then set a match to a pile of wood that I had collected and prepared well before dark. Many fires already flickered up and down the river bank, almost every bend and feature of the river could be made out in their orange and yellow glow. I removed my shoes and pants and placed them as near to the fire as I could to dry them. Ernest removed his rubber waders and produced a pair of shoes from a pack that he had hidden on the bank earlier. He slipped on the shoes and settled in close to the fire, a good log at his back for support. I stood as near to the fire as I could; the chill and damp of the night had begun to set in, and steam rose from my long underwear as I crept ever closer to the fire.

" I don't want to be to forward, and I know that it is really none of my business, but what is it that you do for a living that you can afford chest waders and an L.L. Bean rod?" I asked Ernest.

"I tell stories," he said as the fiery shadows danced upon his face and another big smile flashed from under his huge hat.

There was something about his smile that captivated me. I had recently seen a motion picture in which a young Burt Lancaster threw a similar smile across the screen. Ernest's smile reminded me of Lancaster's; it was a warm inviting smile which gave you the impression that he was your friend and cared for you even if he really didn't. I think Ernest, and even Burt Lancaster for that matter, would have made a great salesman.

"What do you do for a living?" Ernest returned the question.

"Well, I work in my father's mill and fish for these fish; that's all," I said being careful not to reveal too much about myself.

I didn't pay much attention to our small talk and walked over to the tree where the rods leaned and picked up Earnest's rod. He looked up from tying his shoes, and I asked if he minded; he nodded his head and motioned with his hand for me to try it out. I held the rod in my hand, the smooth cork handle snuggled in between my thumb and index finger. I checked above for branches and swung the rod back and forth a few times, it was perfectly balanced. I stripped some line from the reel to test it; the action was smooth. I could see myself fishing with a rod like this someday and told that to Ernest. He, again, nodded his head in agreement and smiled. I sat down by the fire and fondled the rod some more.

Though it may be hard to believe, even the best quality fly rod can get old when there aren't real fish involved. So I placed the rod back against the tree, next to mine. Ernest had taken a leather-bound book from his pack, read through a few pages of it, and then begun to write in it. I asked Ernest what was in the book; he finished the sentences he was working on and looked up.

"It's my journal," he said. "I keep it so that I can remember the details of experiences and, hopefully, draw out the ideas that would make good stories. By the way, how'd you like that fly rod?"

"The rod was great; I hope to own one myself one day," I told Ernest.

"Use the talents that God has given you," he said. "Work hard at whatever skill it may be that was given you, and one day, you will own all that you desire," he looked back down and started writing in his book again.

I stood up and walked to the river bank to listen for the trout. The fires reflected orange off of the river, and men could be heard up and down from our position. Some were talking in low tones; no doubt they, too, were listening for the trout; others spoke in loud voices and laughed hearty laughs. No matter how you went about it, fishing the Hex was fun. I walked back to the fire and found Ernest still writing in his book. It was cool enough now for sleeves, so I walked over to where my things were gathered and grabbed my long shirt, my blanket to sit on, and my guitar. Ernest looked up from his work and chuckled.

"I thought you said you worked in a mill?"

"I do, for money, but I fish and play this for love," I told him.

"You can really play that thing?" he asked, still chuckling under his breath.

I worked myself onto the blanket and began to play an old gospel song I had learned a long time ago when I was a boy. The sweet sounds of the guitar echoed through the river valley and mixed with the crackling of the fires and the babbling of the river. The river darkness was broken by the voice of a man from somewhere up river; he sang the words to the song like he owned them, and Ernest smiled his approval and rocked back and forth in his seat to the rhythm. I strummed the last chord to the song, and a mayfly fell from above onto my hand; I held up my hand to examine the bug against the fire. The hatch was on.

Ernest and I leapt from our seats simultaneously and started for our rods; I left the guitar on the ground near my blanket. Ernest hurriedly kicked off his shoes and donned his waders, and I ran to the river bank; Ernest crept up behind me moments later.

"There," I said turning an ear to the river.

The slurp, slurp of a feeding trout could be heard. We quietly slipped into the water and I whispered to Ernest to make a cast to the trout. The click, click of his reel broke the silence as he slowly stripped line from it. Then the air was ripped apart by his cast, and the fly plopped into the water just up stream from the slurping trout. I instructed Ernest to cast closer to the opposite bank, and when the first drift was well past the slurping sound he lifted the fly from the water and false cast a few times to dry it. I saw the fly drop to the water's surface once again and listened hard; a faint slurp followed, and Ernest set the hook. A mighty brown trout exploded from the water, and Ernest laughed from deep in his chest and sloshed through the water back toward the bank to land it. It was, according to him, the biggest he had ever caught. We spent the next three hours taking turns casting to the feeding trout. I was going to let Ernest catch them all, but he laughed at the thought and insisted that I participate. We talked, we laughed, and when it was over, we dragged ourselves back up the river bank with tired arms from catching so many trout.

We sat back down by the fire where Ernest removed his waders and put his shoes back on. I fashioned a makeshift rack from some green branches and hung my pants over the fire to dry. I begged Ernest to tell me a story; he walked to his pack and brought back a stack of papers bound by a single rubber band.

"I don't tell them; I write them, " he said as he dropped the stack in my lap.

I picked up the papers and began to read; Ernest went back to writing in his journal. It wasn't a long story but it was exquisitely told. It was about the fishing and the country and him and others. He described the scenes so that I could see them vividly in my head, and the story ran me through the gamut of emotion. I raised my head from reading and stared at him; he just continued to write.

"Now," he said, "You know exactly what I do, so do what you should do and play me something on that guitar."

I picked up the guitar and played, but I was just going through the motions, playing another old church song. My mind wondered about the possibilities. I had written a few things down before, lyrics to songs, but I never kept track of them and the napkins got used somewhere along the way. I figured they were silly, but I couldn't get Ernest's words out of my head.

"So do what you should do and play me something on that guitar."

Then, as I strummed, from somewhere down river this time, a different man began to sing to my playing and I made up my mind. Maybe I **should** be playing the guitar and maybe the words I had written were not silly. I played on with renewed enthusiasm and Ernest rocked in his seat, all of the time continuing to write in his journal. I finished playing and set the guitar against a nearby tree; then I got up and put some more wood on the fire.

"Will you write about me?" I asked as I sat back down on the blanket.

"William, you are an intriguing young man. A man who can cast a deadly fly and then play a lovely song when he has finished deserves to be written about," he said, as he closed the journal and placed it back in his pack.

He spread his own blanket and lay down closer to the fire than he had sat.

"I'm paid up through the morning, right?" Ernest asked as he pulled the blanket over his head and rolled over to go to sleep.

"Yes sir," I shook my head to no one as I stared into the fire. I couldn't get the possibilities out of my mind.

"It was a hell of a hatch, wasn't it, William?" was the last thing Ernest said before he drifted off to sleep.

I stayed awake, playing with my guitar and stoking the fire as necessary. I experimented with a few things and made special notes of all of them in my head so that I could write them down later. After a while my legs got stiff, so I got up, with my guitar, and walked down the river past the dying fires. I walked by one fire that was still burning strong and a familiar voice caught my attention. I sat in the company of a friend for the rest of the night; he shared his wine and we sang together as I played. Before I knew it, slivers of orange and blue could be seen to the east and the stars flickered as the light consumed them. I walked back to find Ernest still sleeping near the fire.

I woke Ernest for a morning of fishing; and since there was no breakfast, we did not eat. I was unprepared. Ernest didn't seem to mind, though, and he went about putting on his waders and rigging his rod without complaint. The water had cooled down considerably, and I found myself wishing for a pair of waders like Ernest had, even though I knew the water would warm soon enough, and I'd be glad I wasn't wearing any. Ernest slipped in the river upstream from where I was, and the morning mist again engulfed him. For a moment he was, and to this day still is, a fly fishing river ghost. The orange sun burned his silhouette on my mind as it once again cast its glow about Ernest. It was the big hat and the fly rod that made him stand out. When it was all over, when the mist had burned away and the heat of the day set in, we had caught a few nice trout. Guiding Ernest was an easy task; we spoke nary a word all morning and had had only a few pass between us while we were on the river the night before. It was time to go.

We met on the bank half way between our respective positions and made our way back to the fire. A faint line of smoke rose from the ashes and the left over heat; the fire was all gone. Ernest struggled out of his waders and walked over to me. I extended my hand toward Ernest who placed the L.L. Bean fly rod square in it.

"You'll get more use out of this here than I will where I'm going," he said flashing that smile again from under his hat.

He then took out his wallet and opened it, pushing his fingers through his mustache with his free hand as he thought. He took out some bills and stuffed them in the fingers that I held the L.L. Bean fly rod with. He shook my free hand, said that it had been a pleasure, piled his pack onto his shoulders and started off through the brush.

"And keep playing that guitar," he said as he tilted his head to one side so that the awkward hat would fit between the trees.

Ernest went on to be one of the most famous people of his time, I followed his work quite extensively, even though I never heard from or saw him again after that night we fished the Hex together. From our night on the river I carried three things: The L.L. Bean fly rod, which I still own and fish with to this day; the money, which I squandered and spent frivolously on a good time; most importantly, the courage Ernest gave me to believe in my own work; and the initiative to keep a record of it. It saddened me greatly the day that Ernest left this world; he didn't seem like the type of person who could take his own life. He believed in life and his work too much. However, as I understood it, it was the love of a certain place and the inability to return there that hurt too much. I think the place that he loved was the place where he had no use he for the L.L. Bean fly rod. So he left it here with me, the man who tells stories with his music, to be used on the rivers of his youth.

I fished the Hex alone the summer after Ernest's death. I could picture him there in that big hat as the sun lit up the mist, first in the evening and then again in the morning. During the night I played my guitar alone by the fire and from somewhere down stream, a sweet voice began to sing. This time, though, it wasn't an old song from church; it was one of my songs, a song that was uniquely mine. It wasn't totally mine, though; a piece of it belonged to Ernest. You know the part about creativity and belief, belief in yourself. That morning I woke to a mist that was similar to the one that hung on the water the morning that Ernest and I fished together. I looked up from my fly rod and thought I saw the river ghost standing there in his hat with his L.L. Bean fly rod. I looked closer, though, and realized that it was just courage, and it was everywhere around me, the courage to create, the courage to try.

The Blue Trees

Debra L. Dorosh

Tom paused and stared at the hedge he was trimming as if it had all the complexities of a physics problem.   Despite an hour of clipping, all seemed badly distorted. Frustrated, he wiped the sweat from his brow, picked up the long-handled clippers, and glanced around him. The soft mist of early evening lent the neighborhood a certain air of somnolence. The quiet was punctuated by occasional whirrs of lawn mowers or angry growls of electric lawn edgers which coincided with his mood. This had decidedly been an unnerving day. The anxiety of waiting was wearing him down.

Debra L. Dorosh is presently employed as a junior high school teacher for the Utica Community Schools. Writing is clearly an interest of hers. She enjoys experimenting with prose as well as poetry and is currently working on a mystery novel. Her other interests include political volunteerism and home-improvement projects.

He could still hear the words of the assistant director of the community playhouse, a man who fancied himself cut out for better things than directing amateurs in a converted movie- house-turned community theater. "Good. Good. Thank you for coming tonight. We have a few more auditions to run through and then we'll make our decisions. We'll phone you tomorrow to let you know."

"Funny," he now thought to himself as he gave the offending hedge a vehement whack, "I feel more nervous tonight than when I did my monologue. Maybe it's because I just don't know about amateurs doing Shakespeare of all things."

The real reason for his anxiety he only half-admitted to himself: ever since he had seen the advertisement in the local paper calling for interested persons to audition for roles in the Sandy Creek Community Players production of **A Midsummer Night's Dream**, he hadn't felt the same. What he secretly hoped for was the chance to break the monotony of his life as a furniture salesman and the predictable routine of an otherwise pleasant family life.

"Not that life as a furniture salesman is all that bad," he often philosophically told himself. "In fact, it's been pretty damn good to me." Tom, after all, did possess no small amount of charm, which he could summon at will. He knew instinctively when the frazzled couples with their unruly children in tow were worn to the point where Tom could easily convince them that they couldn't do without the gaudy wares the showroom had to offer. "Yes, Mrs. Johnson," he would begin, "this piece certainly works well with your carpet. Sure, this cotton will wear as well as the nylon. You'll want that with the little sports you have here." He would invariably wink and then tousle the hair of one of the children, who would just as soon kick him, while the harried parents would sign the order on the dotted line. Tom had long ago learned to submerge the guilt he felt for selling the seductive payment plans to people who could scarcely afford the enticements surround them. After all, this was what brought him hefty commissions. Yet all this had of late left him with an aching restlessness at the end of the day and a mad desire to do something, anything, even perform badly acted Shakespeare to take it away.

Tom heard the familiar, guttural sound of his father's car sputter and come to rest in his driveway. That noise on this particular night irritated him. Dropping his clippers to the ground, he hastily bent over in order to remain unseen and began scooping the spent twigs into the clear plastic bags the township now required for lawn refuse. Interaction wasn't what Tom wanted now.

"That's it. That's it. Go on into Shirley," he quietly said to himself. It often seemed she could deal with the old man's ministering better than he. She had a knack of looking up from whatever she was doing, making eye contact, nodding, and then continuing with her task without missing a beat. Perhaps that's why the old man got along so well with her. She was the busy sort.

Keeping busy had always been a philosophy of sorts of his father's. Throughout Tom's childhood, stolen moments of indulgent laziness were rare. "Idleness is the tool of the devil," his father was wont to say, which even then struck the child Tom as odd since his father was one of the least religious men he had ever known. "If you want to keep a kid out of trouble, keep those hands busy!"

Hands. Hands. It seemed it was all he had heard, and that's why he avoided his father now. He couldn't have tolerated this day an inspection of his hedge. He knew from experience his father would find it necessary to pick up a tool not in use at the moment and begin, "If you want this to grow into a nice shape, you need to cut the growth back about this far. Like this." The resulting flurry of activity would naturally impute to Tom that his method of hedge trimming was less than passable.

101

His father certainly wouldn't approve of Tom's new-found interest in community theater. In fact, he didn't seem to approve of the furniture business either. "You know," he would start, "a man's got to be able to look back at the end of the day and see what he's accomplished. A man's got to keep his hands busy." All of this and more would emanate from a man who had spent much of his life bolting bench seats into Dodge sedans as they snaked down the assembly line.

But he wasn't stopping anyway. He merely waved and went into the house, rattling the screen door behind him.

Tom dragged his bag of refuse over to the side of the garage and bent over to release a rabbit from a child-devised prison. As he pulled himself up, he caught his reflection in the darkened garage window. Tom owned, "I guess I can at least see we are looking more and more alike."

His eye wandered to the sidewalk chalk scrawls drawn by his daughter. With a half laugh, Tom thought of his father's painted scrawls on long ago set aside canvas, scrawls Tom never quite understood.

This was a funny thing for Tom to think about now, of all times, when his own creative illusions hung in the balance, but his father's painting had been an unusual interest for a man who seemed beset by a need to keep continually tinkering or building. In fact, his time spent with his paints and brushes had been the only time he didn't keep after his children to stay occupied.

Tom and his sister could watch if they wanted, but their mother would sternly grab one of them by the wrists and say, "Now let your father be for a change." She would silently hand them their crayons and some paper, or Tom would run his Tonka trucks back and forth across the blue braided rug covering the floor of the screened-in porch where all this artistic endeavor took place.   His mother needn't have worried about Tom and his sister, for her husband seemed indifferent to all of them with the compulsive activity replaced by a dreamy-eyed intensity.

Smells of turpentine and oily paint had permeated the air, mingling with the mustiness of the furnishings. Tom would stare, fascinated by smears of blended color that would take shape as florid landscapes that could exist only in fairy tales.

The paintings themselves certainly had puzzled the boy Tom. They reminded him of things that could earn the disapproval of his blue-haired, rosy-cheeked teacher. "Thomas, don't you know," she would begin, placing her gnarled hand over his, forcing him to drop his crayon, "that you can't have green cats?"

Fearful of the wrath of adults, Tom would only nod, "Yes, ma'am." But he would think to himself, "My dad paints things that are funny colors all the time."

That's what the paintings were – composites of nothing as it should be.   Oddly colored objects in strange positions were swathed with bold, thick strokes of paint – strokes that Tom would sometimes lightly touch when no one else was in the room.

Family friends would teasingly say things like, "Van Gogh, don't you want to take a paint brush to the side of your house?" All his father would say was, "Well, you know when you just bolt seats in place all day . . . sometimes I like to do something from scratch."

In time, Tom's father had begun to attract a small amount of local attention, now and then placing a picture in

103

a gallery or small exhibit, places clearly removed from his assembly line world. But what his father had wanted most of all for reasons known only to himself was some recognition for his talents. This desire for recognition became a quest for the blue ribbon for "Best of Show" to be awarded at the On the Town Fall Arts Festival, sponsored by the township's recreation department. All entries would be prominently displayed in the lobby of the huge civic building that set imposingly in the middle of a large piece of acreage not yet surrounded by suburban sprawl. The winner would even get his picture in the local paper.

The coming festival had produced an unmatched spate of activity in his father, resulting in a huge canvas entitled **The Blue Trees**. At first glance, the canvas seemed to present only a visual cacophony of blue strokes, but on closer examination, a dense forest took shape. Tiny people, some beckoning, some threatening, peeked from behind the dense trees, drawing the viewer into the labyrinth. Because of its uniqueness, the painting drew a remarkably predictable reaction from people. Invariably, they would stop, stare, and say in amazement, "My! Look at that! Have you ever seen anything like this before?"

However, on the day of the judging, **The Blue Trees** was positioned on an easel facing the parking lot of the township hall. The coveted "Best of Show" was presented to the sprightly little dentist's wife for her pastel bowl of clumsy flowers. Over the dinner table in what appeared to be an attempt to console his father, his mother had said, "Never you mind. It's just because she has a thing going with one of the judges. Everyone knows. Just to think the way she flashes those eyes and diamonds of hers."

Tom hadn't known what his mother had meant, and when he opened his mouth to ask for an explanation, his mother held him in check with one of her narrow-eyed stares, the kind hawks use when they fix their sights on their prey.

Not seeming to have heard his wife, his father had merely stared at his large, knuckled hands and quietly said, "Well, I guess it's time to put the trees away for now."

And so all the paints and their accouterments were pushed to the back of the old junk closet. Once, a slightly older Tom was fumbling in the closet and came across the collection of paints, now crusting in their tubes. He opened one and squeezed it hard. The paint just crackled in the tube, its viscosity lost. He poked at a few others and noted how all the colors seemed to have lost their brilliancy. He shouted to his mother, "Mom, should I throw this stuff out?"

She had swiftly flown to see what he was doing. "Get out of that closet! Leave those things alone!"

"But why? None of this is any good. Look." He thrust a hardened tube a little too close to her face.

"Never mind! Leave it alone. You don't understand! It's something your father has to know is there. Just in case. Just leave it alone!"

Just in case what? At the time Tom hadn't understood. But as he continued to stare transfixed at the pastel scrawls on the sidewalk, he became dimly aware that the same things that were driving him now also had driven his father.

The ominous gurgling ring of the phone came peeling out to the yard from the house to break his absorption and cause his stomach to flop.

Presently the screen door creaked open and he was

joined by the wizened little figure he had earlier sought to avoid. He only said, "Shirley says to tell you that you didn't get the part." His father looked hard at him and said nothing else.

Tom merely nodded, and as the evening began to settle its blue shapes around them, they, silently and together, whacked at the hedge unmercifully.

To Drown a Memory

Mike VanBuren

Jack Hanford flipped up the collar of his mackinaw jacket and zipped it tight against his neck. The wind and sleet cut viciously at his face as he stared across the rough waters of Higgins Lake.

Damn, he thought, cramming his hands deep into the thick wool pockets. *Is this what it has all come down to? Pauline playing house in her little redwood cabin and me freezing on this godforsaken beach?*

Jack moved behind a clump of gnarled cedar trees to block the relentless northern Michigan wind. It had been blowing hard since he left home that morning, whipping up a cold rain that began to freeze as evening neared.

Mike VanBuren is a communication professional currently living in Kalamazoo. His non-fiction articles have been published in various newspapers and general-circulation magazines, but this is his first attempt at writing fiction. He enjoys traveling and exploring new places with his wife, Dianna, and three children, Anna, Rebekah and Nathan.

He knew it was probably his fault that Pauline had fallen for Larry-What's-His-Name and retreated into the sedate domestic life she so desperately craved. If only she hadn't been so impatient. God knows, Jack had his reasons for not surrendering more of himself to her. But, looking back, they seemed like pretty weak excuses.

                    *   *   *

"C'mon, Jack," a faint voice called over the howling

107

wind. "Stop searching for ghosts and check out this fire. It'll do you more good than standing out in that nasty wind."

Dave Franklin's words jarred Jack from his mental misery and caused his thoughts to come skipping back across the rugged water. "Be right there," Jack hollered at the lone figure kneeling by a small campfire 20 yards behind him. Jack shivered as he took another look across the lake. Then he turned toward the woods. The sweet aroma of fresh-brewed coffee drifted through the trees. It smelled good, he thought, and he needed something to chase away the chill.

Dave looked up as his friend approached the fire. "It's gonna be a cold one tonight," he said.

"No doubt," said Jack, rolling a damp log near the flames and plopping down on it.

Dave reached into a small box near the fire and grabbed a large, tin mug. He poured Jack a cup of steaming, black liquid. Jack wrapped his hands around the warm container and felt the soothing vapors caress his face. It was snowing harder now and the temperatures were falling quickly. Daylight had given way to darkness, and the flames caused eerie shadows to dance off the trees. Dave split another log and tossed the two uneven pieces into the fire.

"There's nothing like a campfire to warm the soul," Dave said as the wood splashed into the red-hot coals and sent sparks spiraling into the night air.

Jack knew how much Dave looked forward to their late-October camping trip in the north woods - a trek they had made each year since they had roomed together a decade earlier at Central Michigan University. Dave always enjoyed the outing, regardless of the weather. A little snowstorm would only make it more challenging.

But Jack wasn't in the mood for any more challenges. Not today. His sense of adventure had all but evaporated that afternoon at a small grocery store near Roscommon, where they had stopped to pick up a few supplies. That's where he had seen her - for the first time in a decade.

*   *   *

Actually, Dave saw the kid first - a pretty blonde girl about 10 years old. "If I didn't know better, Jack, I'd say that girl belongs to you," Dave said matter-of-factly. "She's got your look." Jack laughed at the notion and watched the youngster run across the parking lot to a small, red car.

"That would be Mama," Dave said a moment later, pointing to a tall, fair-skinned woman carrying two paper sacks and trailing several paces behind the girl. "I suppose the kid favors her a bit, too."

Jack pulled his cap low over his eyes and slid down in the seat of Dave's pickup truck. "No way," he said, almost involuntarily. "I'm not believing this."

"Believing what?"

"That's her."

"Who?"

"Pauline."

Dave let out a low whistle and looked quizzically at Jack. "You're kidding me, aren't you?"

"I wish I was."

Jack would have known that cherubic face and determined walk anywhere. It was Pauline all right. She had the same strong body and sharp facial features that always reminded him of actress Meryl Streep, the same soft, strawberry blonde hair he had felt between his fingers countless times.

109

*   *   *

"I think I would have said something to her," Dave said, glancing up at the sullen figure on the other side of the fire.

Jack stared into the flames. He wasn't sure himself why he hadn't at least walked over and said hello. All he knew is that he had been glued to the seat of Dave's truck. Pauline didn't look their way and Jack watched in silence as she put the groceries on the seat of her tiny sedan and climbed behind the wheel.   He remembered his heart pounding wildly, as if it were trying to break loose from his chest, but he was paralyzed by some hidden fear he couldn't name.

Jack took another sip of coffee and slowly shook his head.   "Seeing me would have only reminded her of something she'd rather forget," he said.

"Maybe," Dave said. "But what if she's been thinking about you all these years in the same way that you've been thinking about her?"

Jack yanked some olive-green mittens from his coat pocket and slid them over his hands. He pulled his stocking cap down over his ears, picked up a piece of weathered wood, and tossed it into the flames.

"Fat chance. You're looking at the guy who couldn't even find time to go to Saginaw with her when her dad was dying. And I'm the one who was always rushing her away from my apartment whenever I thought one of my other female friends might drop by."

*   *   *

Jack remembered those days all too well. He was fresh out of journalism school and editing a small weekly newspaper

110

in Grayling. He planned to pay his dues, then break into the world of fiction and become the next Ernest Hemingway. Already he was a local celebrity of sorts and making friends was easy.

One summer evening, Jack was sipping beer and swapping stories with his pals at a small roadhouse near the south branch of the Au Sable River. That's when he stumbled into Pauline's life. He had come to the bar to seek a bit of the old Hemingway mystique in the bottom of a bottle. She had come for a night on the town with her soon-to-be-ex-live-in lover and some friends.

If Jack had known Pauline was shacked up with the stocky man in the denim jacket who was leaning over the pool table, he would never have asked her to dance. That's something he didn't do with another man's woman. Besides, at 26, he wasn't particularly interested in second-hand relationships. He wanted a woman who hadn't been in the sack with every local hustler wearing a plaid flannel shirt.

Pauline didn't mention her bearded roommate until nearly closing time. That's when the exasperated pool player barged into Jack's budding romance to announce that he was leaving with Pauline's friends and that she could find her own way home.

"Never mind him," Jack remembered Pauline saying softly as she nuzzled his neck. "It's over between us. I'm moving out as soon as I can find a place of my own."

It might have been the alcohol, or maybe the chronic loneliness and the feel of her body against his. Jack couldn't really remember. On that particular evening, though, he wasn't concerned that Pauline was a woman with a history that he didn't understand.

She told him that she had been married for three years to her high school boyfriend and had moved north from the Saginaw Bay area when her young husband landed a job with the Crawford County Sheriff's Department. "It didn't work out between us," she said. Before long, Pauline was a 21-year-old divorcee, clerking in a local department store and living in a tiny Roscommon apartment.

But living alone wasn't her style. Within a few months, Pauline had set up housekeeping with one of her ex-husband's best friends. It was merely a partnership of convenience, she said, that quickly soured and left her vulnerable to the first small-time newspaper editor who staggered across the room to introduce her to the Texas Two-Step.

*   *   *

"Well, one thing's for sure," Dave said, invading Jack's silent trance. "There's not much you can do about it now. Better to forget about her and let me set you up with my cousin Mary. I think she's had her eye on you ever since you went with us last year to the big outdoor show in Grand Rapids. She's really a fine lady, you know."

The fire was burning low and Jack stared into the dying embers. "Yeah, too fine for me," he said, swallowing another mouthful of coffee.

Dave raised his eyebrows and looked across the fire at Jack. Both men sat quietly for several minutes, listening to the wind force its way through the dense trees.

"Maybe we ought to put a few more miles behind us," Jack finally said, squinting to see the face of his wrist watch in the dim light. "It's only eight-fifteen. I think we can make the Jordan River tonight."

*   *   *

Jack knew the area around Higgins Lake better than he cared to. It reminded him of things he needed to forget. He thought about the times he and Pauline had come to this same public access site. Sometimes they would sit in his cramped Volkswagen, watching boats and water skiers on the lake. Or they might walk next door to the state park, rest on the playground swings and talk late into the evening. Once they even climbed the fence to the private beach at the conservation school for a moonlight picnic.

Those were good days, he thought. Much simpler than the fast pace he now kept on the city desk of the **Ann Arbor News**. He realized too late that the weeks he had spent with Pauline had been among the best of his days in northern Michigan. He couldn't help but look back on the relationship as a fine gift – one that was his for a season before it withered and blew away like a brightly colored maple leaf dancing in the October wind. And there wasn't anyone to blame but himself. Jack knew he had killed the special closeness they shared with a deadly venom that he had carelessly injected.

He often thought about their long drives through the rural countryside, dodging white-tailed deer and trying to spot fluffy snowshoe hares in the thick underbrush. And he remembered weekends spent at the tiny bungalow Pauline had rented on the west shore of the lake a few days after they met. It was a cozy little nest where they sipped wine, swapped life stories, and listened to Willie Nelson's "Stardust" album for hours on end.

Jack still felt a pleasant sensation deep within whenever he recalled the intense passion between them, the intimate touches they had exchanged in the soft light of Jack's

Grayling apartment, the long kisses on the moon-lit deck of an old pontoon boat anchored 50 yards off the Higgins Lake shore, the warm embraces they shared while lying on a soft blanket in a dark pine forest near the Michigan National Guard camp.

But Jack was just using her. He knew it then and he knew it now. Sure, he had enjoyed her company – probably more than anyone he had ever known. But he couldn't get past her other life - the broken marriage and the faceless men he knew she had given herself to. Jack invested a considerable amount in Pauline, but he also withheld an essential part of himself. Even when he read the card she had mailed him after their first real date - the one that featured an exhausted tennis player and the inscription, "You leave me breathless" - he was unable to say the words she so desperately wanted to hear. After all, he figured that someone more deserving of his attentions would come along.

Jack's secret longings puzzled Pauline, and the emotional distance he kept wounded her more deeply than she would admit. She cried when she made the decision to walk away, but five months with Jack was enough for her to know that they could never be.

*   *   *

"I think the hardest thing about losing Pauline is that I never really saw it coming," Jack said. "If I had known she would give up so soon and so completely ..."

Dave diverted his gaze from the fire. "You could have gone after her," he said.

Jack let out a deep breath and slowly shook his head. "I did, after a while. I was angry at first, though, because she wouldn't return my calls. By the time I cooled off enough to

114

look for her, she had disappeared. Nobody seemed to know where she was, or at least they weren't telling me. Then I heard she was living who-knows-where with another guy, playing nanny to his two kids. I guess I just kind of wrote her off after that."

*   *   *

But forgetting Pauline proved to be difficult for Jack. Sometimes he went a few days without thinking about her. Mostly, though, he found himself wishing she would show up at his door.

Several months after Jack quit his job in Grayling and moved to Ann Arbor, he decided to try finding her again. He took a day off and drove north to the small town in Saginaw County where 18-year-old Pauline Wolfe had graduated from high school 11 years earlier. He couldn't remember at the time just what she had said her maiden name was, so he found a 1971 yearbook in the local high school principal's office and turned the pages until he saw her youthful photograph.

"That's her," he told the helpful school administrator, pointing to the small, black-and-white image. "Any idea whether she has any relatives who still live in the area?"

"I heard that her father died a few years back, but I believe her mother still lives out on Hemlock Road."

Jack hurried from the school and stopped at the first phone booth he saw. He grabbed the tattered directory and tore it open to the "W" section. His finger moved nervously down the small-print list of names. There it was. Henry Wolfe, 7822 Hemlock Road.

Jack remembered his hand quivering as he pushed the first two coins into the round slot on the telephone. The third piece of change was nearly to the phone when it slipped from Jack's hand and clattered to the floor. He bent down, snatched up the wayward dime and shoved it into the hole. Then he held his breath as he dialed the number. It seemed as though the telephone rang for five minutes before he heard a woman's friendly voice.

"Mrs. Wolfe?" Jack said. He swallowed hard and felt a thick lump in his throat. "We haven't met, but I'm an old friend of Pauline's from Grayling. I've lost track of her in recent years. I wonder if you could tell me where she lives."

"Up there in the woods," Mrs. Wolfe said with a soft laugh. "I don't think she'll ever come back home. She and her husband have a darling little house on the south side of Higgins Lake."

Her husband? The words pierced Jack's heart like a broad head arrow launched from a powerful bow, but he tried not to betray his disappointment. "I didn't know she was married. How long ago was that?"

"About ten years now. They have one daughter and are expecting their second child in about a month."

Jack felt the confusion as he scribbled down Pauline's address and telephone number. He told Mrs. Wolfe that he would try to get in touch with Pauline, but he knew that he wouldn't. "If you see her before I do," he said, "tell her I called."

Jack hung up the phone and stared at the quiet receiver. He didn't want to believe it. Yet he knew it was true. He slammed the palm of his hand hard against the phone, then walked slowly back to his car.

*   *   *

The fire hissed and steamed as Dave threw a bucket of cold water on the glowing embers. "Let's get going," he

116

said. "I think the further you get away from this place, the better off you'll be. I'll warm up the truck."

The dark, black night settled around them as the last flame sputtered and died. Jack felt the damp night air rush into his clothing like water through a porous sponge, no longer kept away by the warm flames.

Maybe Dave's right, Jack thought, tossing the final drops from his coffee cup onto the smoldering coals. *Mary is a nice gal. I probably should get to know her better.*

"I'm going down to the lake one more time," Jack hollered at Dave, who was already halfway up the hill to his pickup. Jack stood and stretched his stiff arms toward the treetops, then made his way to the shore.

The fierce afternoon wind had given way to a cold evening breeze, which gnawed at Jack's bare cheeks as he emerged from the shelter of the trees. He walked across the narrow beach and stood at the water's edge. The lights of the homes and cottages on the south shore twinkled and reflected off the lake. He wondered what Pauline was doing and whether she ever thought about him. And he wondered about the young girl he had seen in the parking lot earlier that day.

She doesn't look all that much like me, Jack told himself. *I don't know where Dave got that silly notion. It's crazy.*

Jack had driven by Pauline's cabin many times in the years since Mrs. Wolfe had given him the address. Each time he came north alone, he detoured from Interstate 75 and sneaked around the outer fringes of her world - an anonymous sojourner from Pauline's past wandering aimlessly in search of contentment. He always hoped that he would catch a glimpse of her, perhaps in her yard, or walking along the road. But he never did. Not until today.

The years had been kind to her, he thought. She looked even better than he remembered. The girl was cute, too. And Pauline looked rather content in her role as wife and mother.

Jack smiled grimly at Pauline's memory and scooped up a small, round stone from the sand. He took a final look across the lake and threw the stone as far as he could into the icy water. Then he turned and jogged up the narrow lane toward Dave's truck.

Voices of Michigan

The Zen of Hunting

Rebecca Tavernini

After five phone calls to set it up and another one to say they were running late, my father, brother, and I were headed south to hunt grouse in the tag alder around Arnold. In the way-back of the car, my dad's Ruger over-under and my brother's Remington pump-action shotguns were wrapped in their cases, nestled on a pile of camouflage jackets and hats and blaze-orange vests. Looking over it all, my dad's black-and-white springer spaniel, Mariah, let out an anticipatory whine and did her best to add the true scent of small game hunting to our closed environment, that of dog breath. Beside me rested my loaded Canon 35mm. It had been at least twenty-five years since I had gone on a hunt with these two, although the experience was vicariously available on many autumn nights around the supper table.

As we drove, we talked about my daughter, my brother's son, Mom, NMU's hockey game, speeding tickets, the deer at Presque Isle, how Mountain Dew tastes better in a can... The big and the little. Then the talk turned to hunting.

Rebecca Tavernini worked in the publishing industry for 15 years for book and magazine publishers before starting her own publishing company, Upper Peninsula Publishing. She serves as an editor and freelance writer at *Marquette Monthly* magazine. She lives in Marquette, Michigan with her husband, daughter and son.

Tomorrow's **Detroit Free Press** was to publish an article, written by my father, on "naturalistic hunting": hunting for the experience of being in nature and using primitive equipment in order to level the playing field. He had explained to us what he proposes in the article: setting aside areas for traditional hunting. And why: because he's seen hunting change so much in his lifetime, especially the past twenty years, from participation to domination. The emphasis these days is on bagging the biggest buck or netting the heaviest fish. Equipment and apparatus is so technical that little to no knowledge of the animal or its habitat is required; a boot needn't even get muddy. "I think our resources need respect," he said. "In the past, the emphasis was on the process. We've lost the beauty of the process."

"When I go hunting," my brother, Tom, responded, "I want to shoot my limit of grouse, and when I go fishing I want to catch *big* fish."

"I'm not saying you can't do that," my dad said. "I just think it's best to do it in a way that's honorable and respectful to nature."

He then shared a story of fly fishing on the fabled AuSable River downstate. As he cast his fly, he was thinking of how the Native Americans considered that waterway sacred, and how once the now-extinct grayling fish flashed beneath its golden surface. Across the stream a white pine, 200 years old, had witnessed the coming and going of the loggers. He was thinking what a privilege it was to experience this flowing shrine of Michigan history. Just then a group of young campers and their counselors, armed with inner tubes, appeared on the scene and ran into the river, yelling. "To them," he said, "the AuSable was just a carnival ride."

"Well, we all went tubing down the Apple River in Wisconsin," Tom pointed out. He took the job of devil's advocate seriously.

"The Apple is not the AuSable," Dad replied.

Suddenly we braked hard and made a tight right turn onto a two-rut just past a Speed Limit 55 sign. This dirt road, I learned, is named, Where Charlie Found the Glasses. The moniker refers to a serendipitous experience where Tom and his friend had found a pair of prescription glasses that my dad's hunting partner had lost six weeks earlier.

As they loaded their guns and zipped up their jackets, examined some feathers on the ground, and started off into the woods, I thought about "the process."

With hunting, it's a bit of a ritual, really--the sharing of stories, loading of shells, assessing the area, discussing which way to go. I could see these things had been done the same way time after time.

I stepped gently over some late-blooming strawberry flowers. Even though they wouldn't survive the soon-coming snow, it seemed sacrilegious to squash something so foolishly optimistic. Certainly plants that produce such sweet rubies deserve a touch of deference.

We scrunched through the dried, brown fern and fallen aspen leaves, heading toward "the edge," the place where two ecosystems emerge, the habitat where ruffed grouse dwell, between the tag alders and evergreens. "Some of the young balsams would make fine Christmas trees," I thought. Soon we'd be choosing a holiday tree, sawing a disk off the end of its trunk, then writing "Christmas 1998" on it and adding it to those we've collected over the years. After the tree is decorated and we switch on the lights, it's always satisfying to sit and admire it. But I think it's even more enjoyable getting it that way, remembering the history of each ornament as we pick it from the box, and chart its placement on a branch in relation to the grand scheme of things.

"Look where a porcupine has chewed off the bark on that tree," Tom said to me, pointing up. I saw the blonde wood exposed beneath swaths of gray bark, and a little further down I saw a big clump of porcupine. We got closer and watched him nonchalantly munching away, a plump, prickly Buddha on a branch. *Nothing in nature is identical with what it was the moment before* is one of Buddhism's "Three Signs of Being." The tree, as the porcupine goes on with the process of eating and ingesting the nutrients of the bark, is becoming part of the porcupine. The tree, as it is stripped of its bark is changing, too, unable to protect and transport the nutrients it needs. Yes, they are both different than they were the moment before. As we look at the porcupine and the tree, we are transformed, too. This is now in our memories.

Process connotes transformation, change. It is sometimes a means to an end, like getting the dishes clean, or shooting a ten-point buck. It is sometimes an end unto itself, like breathing, or being out in the woods. Nature's integral process, evolution, isn't something that happened in the past. It is still going on. It's all about slow process, gradual transformation. "The universe and some or all of its parts have undergone irreversible, cumulative changes such that the number, variety, and complexity of the parts have increased. Evolutionism is opposed to the belief that the universe and its parts are eternally the same," states Thomas A. Goudge in the *Dictionary of the History of Ideas*. Is all this to reach an end? That, I guess, is a matter of theology, science, and time. It is a rule of physics, however, that we, the earth, and the universe will not remain the same. Following the laws of thermodynamics, the Earth itself is involved in a process of metamorphosis. As William Thomson wrote in 1852: "Within a finite period of time past, the earth must have been, and within a finite period of time to come the earth must again be, unfit for the habitation of man as at present constituted, unless operations have been, or are to be performed, which are impossible under the laws to which the known operations going on at present in the material world are subject."

I was stepping through what looked like a miniature world: Pine-tree-like club mosses, about the height of my ankle, towered over a city of British soldier lichen, while saw fly moths winged around like tiny seagulls. Nearby, a rough circular sweep of sand spoke of where a grouse had dusted, using its feet and wings to flick gravel into its feathers to groom itself. This impression of a bird come and gone was all we saw here, though. We headed back to the car.

As we pulled into the next spot, along the Ford River, Dad mentioned woodcock hunters he had guided here. Many places, it seemed, were habitated with more than the physical flora and fauna. I imagined the gentle conversation between my dad and the other hunters as they passed this same wide oak that an enthusiastic but eventually defeated beaver had left its mark upon. Along the river, I noticed a rusted, metal, card-table-type chair perched on the bank in a lovely spot. What memories paint this place in other minds?

The woods gave promise, with grouse and woodcock droppings splattered on the fallen leaves. Mariah's tail started wagging in a fixed time and her nose took to the ground. It looked like she meant business. We watched her intently, on alert for the lawn-mower hymn of a flushed grouse or the whirlwind whistle of a woodcock's wings. In anticipation, Tom took a few practice swings with his gun. Mariah then picked up her nose and trotted over to us. Apparently, it was just another memory, a scent left behind by a bird no longer here.

As we made our way under archways of white, climbing virgin's bower that looked like shooting stars frozen in time, we remained ready for a flush, but paused to look at the geometry of a fallen tree's roots or the mark of a buck's rubbing. We came upon deer hair scattered like down feathers across a quilt of moss beneath an evergreen's umbrella. An alveolus in the moss nearby indicated where a carnivorous creature had rested and enjoyed a meal. We could find no bones, and speculated as to what had happened, and where. The story, however, had already been told. We just happened by and experienced some of it, like reading a few pages from the middle of a book. In a few weeks the scene would be hidden by snow. But right then, we took it in, and it changed us.

Dusk was on its way, but we thought we'd try one more spot. As we drove in, a pileated woodpecker swooped in front of us. Then the ritual of loading the guns and setting the course. The good sound and smell of crunching leaves. Dad and Tom were starting to get embarrassed that we hadn't even seen a game bird yet. "That's all right, I thought, for Jack Kerouac, it wasn't the destination, it was the journey. Toying with my other thoughts of transience and change, I remembered a quote from Kerouac: "Everything comes and goes. How good it is!"

We stepped over a narrow gully and Dad explained

that it was a fire break dug during a wild fire that had blazed about thirty years ago, he guessed, by the size of the trees. We went up an incline and he related how he had once shot a woodcock right here, on his way in, and one right here, on his way out. We walked over to a broad, brown marsh with a big, old beaver lodge. Judging from the dead cedar sentries, the beavers that had built the lodge and dam, and several succeeding generations of beavers, had changed the essence of this area. Mariah ran down to drink from the slow stream winding through it like a thread of time.

Dad called in three gray jays having a raucous conversation. They perched on the naked trees overhead, studied us briefly, and went on their way. As Dad and Tom unloaded their guns and took off their camo, they assured me that this was the only time in their lives that they'd gone hunting and not flushed a single grouse or woodcock, or at least seen one from the car. Unfortunately, I thought, the next time they hunted these spots they'd probably think of them as the place Where We Didn't See Any Birds At All When Becky Came Along. They talked about the odds of that as we followed the road home while the day turned to night.

"All we are is the result of what we have thought," Buddha whispered in the passing wind.

We didn't have a bag of birds in the back, but we did have a day to remember.

Voices of Michigan

Paul Bunyan's Brother

Daniel Suits

Paul Bunyan was the hero of many tales told around a hot stove of a winter evening in the old logging camps; he was, of course, a character of folklore. But sixty years ago, when I worked with the U.S. Forest Service on the Manistee National Forest in Michigan, I knew a man who might have been Paul Bunyan's younger brother, except that he was a real person, and I can attest to his deeds.

Daniel Suits taught Economics for 43 years. He is the author of several books and technical articles on economics, but since retirement he has been writing for a more gen-eral audience. His re-cent publications in-clude pieces in environmental maga-zines and airline in-flight magazines.

The first time I set eyes on Hjalmar, he was heaving on one end of a six-foot, two-man, cross-cut saw felling oak timber for railroad ties. He was tall, slim and lithe, and at first sight didn't appear unusually muscular, but appearance was belied by the effortless power he applied to the saw and by the sweating struggle of his partner on the other end.

It didn't take long to realize that Hjalmar was the strongest man I had ever met. When not cutting timber, he was the blacksmith of the camp and prided himself on his ability to lift his anvil by the horn with only one hand.

Hjalmar combined this strength with enormous confidence in himself. I once watched him lift a five-gallon pot of boiling water off a huge, waist-high, wood-fired kitchen range and lower it gently to the floor. This was not braggadocio, but merely the performance of a task that had to be done. We needed the pot on the floor. He put it there for us. In fact, Hjalmar was genuinely modest about his strength. "You may t'ink aye am strong," he would often say in his soft Swedish lilt, "but, man alive, you should see my brother. Is *he* strong!"

But Hjalmar was known for many things beside sheer strength. For example, he had many beautifully knitted sweaters and seemed to wear a different one every day. When anybody remarked on one of them, he would explain, "Oh, my girlfriend, Hulda in Minnesota, made this for me." The next day it would be, "Oh, my girlfriend, Ingrid, made this for me." And so on throughout the week. "In Minnesota," he would remark, "there are many, many pretty girls."

Hjalmar had a pleasant singing voice and, accompanying himself on the guitar, could yodel as well as any country singer, yet he had never taken music lessons. He had heard country music on the radio (there was no television in those days), thought it sounded like something he would like to do, bought a guitar, and taught himself to play and sing.

Although I never saw Hjalmar with a book or even a newspaper, his handwriting was extraordinary. Somewhere he had seen examples of Spenserian script and had so admired the graceful sweep of the letters and the elaborate swirls and curlicues that he immediately set about practicing by himself.

I never saw the inside of any of his letters to Hulda and Ingrid, but the envelopes were addressed in perfect, flowing, Spenserian script. When visitors stopped by the camp office, the mail clerk took pride in picking Hjalmar's letters from the outgoing box to show them "how our blacksmith writes."

Ultimately, I learned that even as a blacksmith Hjalmar was self-taught. No doubt he had seen smiths at work, but he had never worked in a smithy or been trained to the trade. As I got the story, a logging chain snapped one day, and a repair was urgently needed.

"Does anybody here," the foreman asked the assembled crew, "know anything about smithing?"

Hjalmar immediately stepped forward. "Why, I am a blacksmith."

Taking the chain, he went into the smithy, carefully shut the doors against prying eyes, lit the fire, and experimented until he could make a satisfactory weld. He presented the foreman with the repaired chain and was forthwith designated camp blacksmith.

Although he was never bashful about his ability, Hjalmar never boasted, nor did he ever bluff. When Hjalmar said he could do something, however wild and unlikely, it was heavy odds on that he could. One time some of us were passing time in the smithy when Hjalmar, rummaging through a box of small junk, came across a handful of little staples.

"I bet you," he said, fingering one of the staples, "that I can throw this staple and make it stick on the wall." He turned and threw the staple, but it bounced off the wooden wall and clattered across the floor.

"Oh," he said, "I am too close."

He stepped back a few inches and threw a second staple. It stuck in the wall. He followed it with another, and, as I recall, decorated the wall with seven staples in succession.

He again searched in the box and found a large staple, the kind that might serve as hasp for the padlock on a barn door. He pointed to a short length of board lying in one corner. "Here, Rudy," he said to one of the men, "stand over there and hold out that board."

Rudy duly picked up the board and held it straight out at arm's length at the designated spot, thumb in front, fingers behind. Hjalmar wound up and fired the staple at the board. Not only did the staple stick, it bracketed Rudy's thumb. If the staple had been driven with more force, his thumb would have been stapled to the board.

Hjalmar could hardly contain his excitement. "I was trying to do that! I was trying to do that!"

And who am I to say he wasn't?

Once, after a heavy snowfall, Hjalmar and I were trudging through the woods on snowshoes when we scared up a rabbit. I remarked it was too bad we didn't have a gun, we could have rabbit stew for supper.

"We don't need a gun," Hjalmar said, "we'll just run him down on foot."

It sounded ridiculous, but I soon saw he was right. In the first place, since the rabbit left tracks in the snow, he couldn't lose us and hide. In the second place, the rabbit didn't run in a straight line, but zigzagged, so by going straight ahead, we had less ground to cover than he did. Finally, although rabbits are quick over short distances, they can't keep up the pace and must pause frequently to recover breath.

We steadily gained ground on the rabbit and could easily have caught him except for one thing. He knew the woods better than we did. Just when we were ready to grab him, he popped into a hollow tree with a ground level opening. We reached into the hole, but couldn't touch him. So much for rabbit stew.

But nothing Hjalmar ever did matched the feat I saw him perform the afternoon we went to help a neighboring farmer. The farmer kept a few chickens which he allowed to run free in a large yard. This undoubtedly added to the flavor and nutrient value of meat and eggs, but an obvious downside became apparent when the farmer began to chase a rooster he intended for supper. Each time he got the rooster cornered and lunged for the capture, the bird escaped in a flurry of squawks, dust, and feathers.

Hjalmar watched for a few minutes and then called out, "Have you got a gun?"

The exhausted farmer drew up and glared. Of course, he had a gun, but he wanted chicken for supper, not a skillet full of buckshot.

"No," Hjalmar said, "I mean have you got a twenty-two? I will shoot his head off."

Rooster or no rooster, this was something the farmer had to see. He went into the house and brought out a twenty-two caliber rifle which he handed over. Hjalmar inspected the rifle, raised it to his shoulder, and followed the rooster's dash across the other end of the yard. One shot, blam! The astonished farmer picked up the bird and carried it into the house. A minute later, he emerged with a half dozen empty beer bottles.

"Here," he said, "see if you can hit this." And he tossed a bottle into the air.

Hjalmar fired and shattered the bottle. One after another he broke five bottles, but the sixth fell untouched. "Oh," he said, twirling his hands to illustrate, "I thought it was going to turn this way, and it turned that way."

The farmer tossed the bottle again, and that time it must have turned as expected, for it met the fate of the others.

All this was long, long ago. But nobody I have met since has come even close to matching Hjalmar's strength, ability, skill, curiosity and enthusiasm for life. He may not have been Paul Bunyan's brother, but Hjalmar was unique.

Moving Cloud

Amy J. Van Ooyen

She might have come wandering along the old logging road to our clearing in the forest.

Approaching me from the direction of the pond, she spoke in a quiet, assuring manner saying, "I am an Indian."

She was caressing a white feather with her strong, tanned fingers. The large pin-feather undoubtedly was found near the pond from one of our geese, a gander that lost it in a fight with a wild animal that had killed his mate. Softly moaning, the gander's questions were unanswered, but only mirrored by a lonely reflection in the pond.

Amy J. Van Ooyen was honored as the 1992 writer of the Upper Peninsula of Michigan. She has written for several magazines and nature publications. She also has published three books of life near the lakes and in forests of the Upper Peninsula: *Live it U.P., Now and Then in the U.P., Creatures and Characters in the U.P.* Also, *Transplants* was published in December 1998.

Unsure of the woman's intention and a little uneasy, I waited for her to speak. She did not until she reached in her pocket and laid a green pebble on the railing of our deck, saying, "This belongs here."

I wanted an explanation of her unusual gift, but she instead seemed pleased to notice my confusion smilingly waiting for my response.

I know green stone is the ancient bedrock protruding near the mouth of fast flowing rivers in to Lake Superior. She might have taken this beautiful stone from the beach near Little Girl's Point where it is found in contrast with many other rocks and pebbles.

"Yes," she said, "I am an Indian and also a Christian," chuckling timidly, as if she thought it a contradiction.

"Welcome to our home." I invited her to come in; maybe she would tell more about herself.

Accepting immediately, she told me she had taken a drive down our dead-end road while exploring the area. Our driveway was blocked by a car, but the flowers growing in our backyard and the goose drifting on the pond had attracted her. She had taken a footpath, walked past our vegetable garden and waited until our visitors left.

"I've been teaching for four days at the 4-H Extension Camp at Little Girl's Point," she said. "It is a youth seminar sponsored by several churches in the Upper Peninsula of Michigan and Northern Wisconsin. We teach Indians and Whites about our culture." It explained her dual loyalty.

She motioned to our garden, complimenting us that we had a nice place here in the forest.

"We do like living here," I said. "We have a love for the land."

"At one time, our tribe owned all this land. The territory was reaching from the border of Illinois to the shores of Lake Superior." The pride in her heritage was unmistakable. "I've been away from our tribe, but I've returned to my people living in Central Wisconsin. My home is large and it gives shelter to several members of my tribe who, unfortunately, need special care. Keeping busy is the best therapy to stay healthy and happy. I make everyone work."

She chuckled about her stern philosophy of life, and the glimmer in her eyes convinced me of her inner strength.

"We are foreigners, actually like a weed that blew on this soil; we took hold and grew, then prospered," I said.

She understood my symbolizing language and nodded.

"I know you belong here; it's the reason for giving you that green stone. Yes, you speak my people's language, and I will show you something I made." When she returned from her parked car with a beautiful basket, she told me of its beginning. "I had a fear of making this, thinking it could not be done by me. This basket was not to have a flaw in it. Not even the smallest flaw. This is my first attempt of making a basket, and there will not be another like it." She was serious now, looking at me anxiously for a response.

"You have great skill," I said. "This is a beautiful example of art. Why will there not be another one?"

My question surprised her; then trusting me, she began to tell me about her grandmother who had been known in the tribe for her beautiful baskets, woven from strips of black ash trees, bleached and later colored by natural dyes.

With a touch of pride in her voice, she said, "I've made this basket in her memory; therefore, it was to be perfect."

I was awed by her traditional dedication and deep reverence for her ancestors.

Opening the treasured basket, she showed me one of the soft leather pouches an Indian medicine man wears.

"I've told the children about our medicine men, and we've been making pouches, filling them with gifts of the good earth. The Great Spirit gave us many healing herbs and several plants which our wise medicine men recognize, having knowledge of good and evil."

I told her that a former neighbor, also an Indian, had told me about the benefit some plants have. "There is one that soothes the pain of fractured bones. He made a poultice and placed it directly on my badly bruised wrist after a fall. This man told me of a tiny, leafy herb which often grows in moss near a tree that will relieve a toothache, and also eases the discomfort of a teething baby by rubbing it on the gum. But he gave me a warning. One must use it sparingly, for there is danger when one applies too much. A person's heart beat may slow down and cause death. I have taken pitch from bulging areas on the bark of balsam trees, at his suggestion. It is a sticky mess, but it draws out an infected wound and also relieves the terrible itch of black fly bites."

My limited medicinal knowledge encouraged the Indian woman. She grappled at the bottom of her basket and pulled out a very small leather pouch. This one did not have fringe like the larger ones. Then from under her clothing she took another like it, hanging from a leather strap around her neck.

"In this pouch is a small stone," she said.

I looked at the worn amulet when she now, seriously, again assured me that she was a Christian. "I don't believe in this, but we Indians say the stone in this pouch will ward off evil spirits."

"I am also a Christian," I said. "We don't have to fear evil spirits."

Replying immediately, her voice lowered and motioning at possible forces around her, she whispered in a husky voice, "But there are evil spirits."

"Yes, there are. Sad to say, this is true, except you and I don't have to be afraid. Our God came to the rescue. He is mightier than all those who try to harm us, by giving us Jesus, His Son."

Her eyes at once lit up, and she said, "I tell you my name in my language. It is Monge-Won Quot. It means 'Moving Cloud'".

Introducing myself, I told her, "You have a beautiful name."

Her temperament changed quickly, like a cloud from happiness to serious, thoughtfulness and joy. Still holding the small pouch in her hands, she now excitedly told me, "You have an Indian name also. I could feel it when I came to your garden and I am sure of it. Your name came to my heart. Yes, I am very sure."

Pressing one index finger firmly on my chest, she ceremoniously draped the leather strap with the tiny pouch that held a stone, around my neck, saying solemnly, "Your Indian name is Earth Mother."

Smilingly waiting for my approval, her dark brown eyes revealed her having one more surprise for me. Pressing now her index finger on the pouch, Moving Cloud gave me her beautiful dual blessing, that of an Indian and of a Christian.

"God bless you, Earth Mother. May the Great Spirit, Jesus, be with you in the rising of the sun, in the dew of the garden, in the smile of an animal, in the warmth of your husband and in your many friends and loved ones."

When Moving Cloud left me, I understood the awesome meaning of her gift, a green stone. Only a chip of the oldest bedrock on earth, chafed, punished and polished by sand, gravel and waves of Lake Superior. I was certain I would find a second green stone in my little pouch, but was surprised to find a tiny rectangular quartz, clear as crystal. Shining like a diamond, a ray of sunlight made its facets sparkle, revealing the true miracle of God's love for all His people. I realized that I, Earth Mother, with Moving Cloud, existing here on earth by God's grace, belong to Heaven.

Paper or Plastic?

Stu Stuart

Paper or Plastic?

Neither. We prefer boxes, please.

One of the first things you learn when living on Mackinac Island is paper or plastic bags just won't do when it comes to getting large amounts of groceries safely to

> **Stu Stuart** is a summer resident of Mackinac Island and a stand-up comedian. In the winter, he lives in Los Angeles, California.

your home. With no privately owned automobiles on the Island, even daily tasks such as getting groceries to your home becomes an adventure.

This groceries-in-a-box concept is one of many survival skills necessary to live on Mackinac. And you won't read about it in any book at any price. It's just one of those things that long-time Islanders know, and newer ones, such as myself, usually learn about the hard way.

You only have to have your groceries strewn across a ferry luggage cart, dock, or street once to know you have exercised poor judgment in your choice of grocery containers.

If you ever see anyone bringing groceries to the Island in open bags, they are either first timers, new, or slow learners.

The good folks who run the grocery store on the Island and those in St. Ignace, in most instances, are experts at packing your groceries in boxes. There's an art to it. You just can't put all the canned foods in one box or you'll need a forklift to carry it. You also have to be careful not to crush bread or chips.

And transporting cold items such as milk and ice cream can present a challenge, too. The solution: a cooler. Works perfect to keep those perishable items cold, fresh and in their original shape.

When it comes to boxes, not just any old one will do. It has to have a lid and preferably be a banana box although some people prefer egg boxes. Banana boxes are sturdy, generally crush proof, can withstand a pretty good rain storm, and fit nicely in a bike basket or garden cart which are the main modes of getting groceries home.

Whatever the box, always write your name on it with a marker in large letters. With dozens of these boxes of groceries arriving on the Island each day, you want to make sure no one accidentally absconds with your frozen pizzas, pickled pigs' feet or lifetime-supply of dental floss.

Be careful if you decide to go to Cheboygan, Petoskey or the Soo for groceries as they are generally unaccustomed to the ritual of boxing groceries. Asking for a box can bring the entire store to a grinding halt as the staff organizes a posse to find the outlaw boxes holed up in some back room or alley. Then, two days later after they find the boxes and the angry people in line behind you have strung you up by your ankles, the baggers have no clue as to how to properly pack your groceries.

They don't understand that as Islanders, we need boxes! And we need them now because we're in a hurry to catch a ferry. So there is no time to give the history of grocery boxing to the uninformed bagger. "Never mind, *why* I need boxes—no time to explain—must go—now! Just get me some boxes, no one gets hurt, and I shall leave peacefully."

142

In fact, a good rule of thumb is don't bring anything to the Island that you value in an open bag. The odds are just too great it will tip over, rip, get crushed, be run over by horses, or be shot out of a cannon. And when it comes down to it, why take that chance? Have you ever seen a watermelon shot out of a cannon? Me either, but that's neither here nor there.

My point is, always ask for boxes when you go on major grocery shopping expeditions; this way you will never have to suffer the humility of having to explain to dinner guests why your bread looks like soft tortilla shells.

Voices of Michigan

Ernest Hemingway Sat Here

Ellen W. Rosewall

I am sitting in a wicker chair. It is an unassuming chair, the kind found on the front porches of cottages like ours up and down the lake. It's an antique, probably over ninety years old; it sags a little, and a couple of loose ends of rattan threaten to break free and poke me in places I do not wish to be poked. But it is the perfect place to read a book and watch a sunset.

I am reading a book. It's an unassuming book, and it too is old, but younger than the chair. It

Ellen W. Rosewall has written fiction for many years in the form of public relations and fundraising materials. *Sparkle Island*, from which *Ernest Hemingway Sat Here* is taken, commemorates the 100th birthday of her summer cottage on Walloon Lake and will be published by Raven Tree Press in the spring of 2000.

is a book that sits in libraries, classrooms, and homes around the world, widely admired and celebrated. It is a book written by a man who once sat in this chair. Maybe.

Our summer cottage on Walloon Lake has been in the family for seventy years now, but before my Grandfather bought it in 1930, it was owned by two brothers from Marion, Indiana, named William and Walter Siddons, AKA "Windy Bill" and "Gloomy Gus." Although Walloon was not nearly as populous as it is today, the Siddons had several neighbors, including a family a couple of miles down the road whose youngest child is the subject of this story.

Now, it seems that in those days it was somewhat of a coup to lay claim to the fastest boat on the lake, and for several years, the Siddons held that honor. Their beautiful launch, **Onward**, had one of the first gasoline powered engines and was reputed to travel as fast as thirty miles per hour. This incredible feat earned them the duty of being fire marshals, traveling up and down the lake in times of emergency, notifying neighbors and collecting whatever resources, human or otherwise, were necessary for the occasion. When guests stepped into the boat, they sat on the wicker chairs that were the fashion for upscale launches of the day – the same wicker chairs that now sit on our front porch.

These things we know. What we do not know, but what we imagine, is that during one of the aforementioned emergencies, Windy Bill and Gloomy Gus hopped in the boat and went off searching for help. Stopping at Windemere, they were greeted by a gentleman and his young son. "Can I come, too?" asked little Ernie Hemingway. "Sure, hop in," said Windy Bill, and so the young lad clambered into the boat, eagerly claiming one of the wicker seats in the rear so he could watch lake and shore at the same time. The chair creaked a bit as Ernie leaned over to trail his fingers in the water, and while the adults were planning their rescue mission, stories of lakes and trees were spinning in Ernie's head. Once the emergency was over, the boat stopped back at the Siddons' and Ernie climbed up and down the broad steps of our front porch while the men relaxed, had a beer, and enjoyed the sunset.

For most of my life, this tenuous connection to a famous writer has fueled my imagination in what I hoped was the same way our cottage fueled Ernie's. I dreamed that when Ernie sat on our chairs or climbed up our steps, it started a spark that would manifest itself in a story many years later. I hoped that something of that spark would also manifest itself in my stories; that the lake which had birthed one writer would be gracious enough to inspire another.

The truth is a little less romantic. There is no record of anyone in my family actually having any contact with the Hemingways after my grandfather purchased the cottage. For many years, the Hemingway cottage was occupied by Ernest's sister Sunny, who was, to use the media parlance, a "private person." We never met her, nor did we ever see her on any of our walks down the back road past her cottage although she did surface every once in awhile to publish a memoir or poetic tribute to the lake she loved as much as we do.

Sunny passed away a few years back, and her son, Ernest Hemingway Mainland, inherited the cottage. We heard a rumor shortly afterward that he was going to restore the cottage to the way it was when his uncle lived there, and we waited for the other shoe to drop, anticipating the diesel smell of the tour busses heading down our little road. But, thankfully, our fears turned out to be unfounded. Ernie Mainland opened the house to the public for a brief period when he assumed ownership, and again on the occasion of Hemingway's 100th birthday in 1999, but aside from that, Windemere has remained a private cottage.

147

We know that Ernest Hemingway is a public figure, but we have been grateful that Walloon and Windemere have remained for some reason largely untouched by the media mania that seems to have affected every aspect of the private lives of other famous people. Certainly one of the reasons we are grateful is that Walloon is our retreat, and we don't want it spoiled by traffic and gawkers. But hidden beneath that are the secret fantasies of our family's theoretical brush with greatness that we have held onto for so many years and don't want to let go. We love to take our guests on a walk or drive and dramatically announce in hushed whispers that we are passing Ernest Hemingway's cottage as they search in vain for some kind of indication that we are correct (we're residents here, we just *know*). And the possibility definitely exists that if Ernie Mainland had thrown open the doors of Windermere, it would also have thrown open the doors of history to closer scrutiny, and we would have found evidence that shattered all of our childhood myths of close ties between Ernie's house and ours.

Ernest Hemingway was a writer who embodied the axiom, "write what you know." After years of reading his terse, direct style, I admit that he would probably disapprove of my creating fanciful legends of something in our cottage inspiring one of his stories. I do have some consolation, however, in the fact that those chairs from the boat are very real. When I sit in one, it's hard not to imagine the thought of wicker marks on that famous backside all those years ago.

A Berry Good Lesson

Sharon Lee Maloney

The day was as perfect as any day could possibly be. We quickly found our secret spot in the woods, the familiar place we return to each year about the middle of July. The only sounds I could hear on that perfect day were birds chirping and wind blowing through the tops of the pines. My daughter and I searched beneath the ferns for the prized blueberry plants that seem to magically appear throughout Northern Michigan's woods every year without the help of a gardener, fertilizer, or pesticide. God is the Master Gardener of the hundreds of acres of wild berries which grow abundantly in our beautiful state. We began our treasure hunt and foraged for only a few seconds before we found our treasures.   There they were, faithful as a hundred years ago when early settlers hitched their horses, loaded their families into their wagons, and headed for the woods during blueberry season, or huckleberry harvest as they referred to the event. They picked for a week or so, depending upon that year's bounty, which depended much upon the temperatures and amount of rainfall. The berries were then sent by train downstate and sold to those not so fortunate as the local

Sharon Lee Maloney's passion for writing began around age seven when she discovered that the 26 letters of the alphabet could be manipulated to create words. She was born and reared in Detroit and now resides near the small Northern Michigan town of South Boardman with her husband and four children.

residents who had access to the bountiful crop of wild berries, free for the taking. As I knelt picking berries, it seemed I could almost hear the echoes of the children playing after a hard day of picking, the sound of the horses' hooves, the mother calling the family for supper. My thoughts sprung back to the present day when I heard my daughter call out, "Oh my goodness, Mommy! Come and look at these!"

Hanging like little clusters of grapes that hovered only inches above the sandy, pine needle-covered ground, these luscious looking blueberries were begging to be picked. We gently and meticulously rolled the small, beautiful blue gems between our fingers and thumbs and watched them pool into our greedy palms. They made soft, plopping sounds as we gingerly dropped them into our plastic ice cream pails. We felt like singing, so we sang a while. When we felt the urge to taste, we did, even though we knew we could easily eat up our entire harvest in just a few moments. Thoughts of blueberry milk shakes, blueberry muffins, and blueberry pancakes, saved us from certain gluttony.

Our pails slowly filled and we considered leaving, but we always found that to be the most difficult part. Suddenly a sight that would have made a photographer quiver caught my attention. Two medium-sized pine trees stood about a foot apart. Nestled between them were two blueberry plants, loaded with perfect berries. In the forefront stood three mushrooms that varied in height like stair steps, each one slightly smaller than the one to its left. A few small stones lay before them upon brown pine needles, and the backdrop was a carpet of dark green ferns. The late afternoon sun filtered through the trees casting soft shadows mixed with streams of sunlight that moved slightly over the ground as the breeze swayed the treetops. I stretched out on the ground so my mind could absorb at eye level the scene which lay before me. I wished I could have dug everything up just as it was and taken it home with me, so I could cherish it forever. I wished I could freeze that moment of time. Never before had anything I'd ever seen in nature touched me like this. Not a mountain, or a waterfall. Neither a magnificent old oak tree, nor a patch of snowy white Trilliums. I wondered why it made such an impression. I gazed at the spectacular scene, afraid to touch, almost afraid to breathe or to blink lest it would go away before I could fully appreciate its beauty. I regretted not having a camera, though I knew that even Kodak couldn't capture the beauty, the colors, the lighting, or the shadows exactly as I saw them at that moment through my own eyes.

We finished picking our blueberries and drove home, but I couldn't stop thinking about the mushroom and blueberry scene. I tried to tell several people about it, but they either stared at me like I was insane or gave an appeasing smile, or exerted great effort to even listen. It became clear to me that anyone who had not seen it couldn't really understand, no matter how vivid and precise my description. But then, has anyone ever described a sunset so eloquently as to match its true splendor?

The following day the scene was still on my mind, and I knew I had to go back with a camera and at least attempt to capture it on film. Because I wanted an exact replica of yesterday's scene, I waited until late afternoon so the lighting would be the same as when I'd made my discovery.

"It will be perfect," I told myself. "I'll have the picture enlarged and framed, and I'll hang it someplace where I can look at it often and be reminded of the happiness that filled my heart just yesterday. I'll send copies off to magazines," I thought. "I'll enter my picture in the county fair, and share it with anyone who wants to appreciate true beauty."

My nephew graciously lent me his new camera equipped with a zoom lens. I imagined I could get so close that I could easily count the legs of a gnat resting on the middle mushroom. I was determined to get the picture, and a part of me needed to have it come out right.

I drove along the winding dirt road with great anticipation of a successful, though amateur, photo session. I easily located the two pines that grew so close together they offered shelter to the blueberries and mushrooms. I leapt from my car and eagerly knelt before the spot where nature's remarkable beauty had entrapped me just the day before. But an intense disappointment swept over me when I saw all that remained. I stared in disbelief. What had happened? I began to feel tears stinging in the corners of my eyes when I saw that the mushrooms had shriveled so badly they were almost non-existent. Several blueberries had fallen from their branches and lay wasting on the ground, and those still hanging on appeared dried and wilting. The dark green carpet of ferns now had brown on the edges of their curling leaves. The lighting wasn't right, and the shadows weren't right. How could this be? How could everything have changed so drastically from yesterday?

Since I had made the effort to return, I snapped a few pictures anyway, but was disheartened by the fact that my prints wouldn't even come close to portraying what was there only 24 hours earlier. Knowing I could never go back and experience that moment again in exactly the same way, I became angry. Was there something to be learned from this? If so, I sure couldn't see it at the time.

One of the few positive qualities I've possessed for as long as I can remember is that of being optimistic. In fact, I was elected "the most optimistic" by my senior class, an honor which has, admittedly, been difficult to live up to at times. I've tried to look at the brighter side of things, often looking for a positive lesson to be learned or insight to be gained even in the inconsequential things in life. Yet, at that moment, I couldn't find a brighter side, much less a lesson or valuable insight, and I wondered if God might be trying to teach me something through this disappointing experience. I questioned why He hadn't allowed my picture-perfect spot in the woods to remain as it was for just another day. Surely He knew how happy it made me, and He knew I wanted to get a picture so I could retain the memory. Why, then?

With a deep sigh, I succumbed to the fact that life itself continually changes and nothing I could have done would have preserved the perfect scene in the woods for even one more hour. I had a brief feeling of helplessness and insecurity. Flickering through my mind came thoughts of people I know who seem perfectly healthy one day, and get a diagnosis of cancer the next. A loved one at your side one moment may be taken in a heartbeat, never to be held again in this life. The death of a beloved pet. The marriage of a grown child. A job transfer, a car accident, a divorce. Sudden unemployment, unexpected bills, a fire, a heart attack or stroke, a friend or family member moves away, and suddenly your life is never the same.

Instantly and gently the lesson came. Perhaps the Lord thought I needed a reminder about being grateful, because, like the mushrooms and blueberries, the things and the people I love and enjoy today may be gone tomorrow. How important it is to cherish the time I spend with my children, to be thankful for loving embraces, to appreciate good times and laughter shared with friends, and not take for granted good health, a sound mind, the ability to work and to pick berries. I realized that someday these things would be the memories to which I'd cling. These would be the memories that would keep the spark lit inside my soul and bring refreshing happiness on the darkest days. Someday, I would refer to these days as the good ol' days.   Realizing that my life is like a vapor that will soon vanish, I thank God that He cares about us enough to teach us lessons along the way. Sure, we should take time to smell the roses. But let's not forget to take time to hug our children, care for our parents, encourage our friends, help our neighbors and praise our God. Let's find time to pick blueberries and sing, and not be blinded to the beauty that lies around us, or the lessons we can learn along our journey.

Wise Woman

Roger Leslie

Wise woman, my grandmother. Baka (a mispronunciation of the Polish "Babcia" that remained with her forever) became one of the first residents of Dearborn Heights long before I was born. By the time I was old enough to weave my experiences with Baka into the tapestry of who I was, the sidewalks of Drexel were already pockmarked, and the cherry tree she'd planted spread above her back yard so wide and dense it blocked the sun from her lawn so that the grass only grew in patches.

I was never much of a daredevil as a child, but I could climb that tree like nobody. It was as if the tree had grown just to accommodate me. By the time I was eight, the main trunk split right at chest level to me, so hopping up and getting a secure foothold was effortless. Four distinct branches could support me all the way to the top, if only precariously, and I would go up, up, up until I was so high I could see clear across four yards in either direction.

When Baka would come looking for me, she had to crane her neck and squint to distinguish me amid the cluttered leaves. "Your mother would kill me if she saw you that high. Get down from there."

As I worked my way down, she instructed, "Stay where the branches are sturdy and can support you. Never risk your fate to an unpredictable wind."

Once I reached the branches that didn't bow from my weight, clustered cherries dotted the green surroundings like

155

a Seurat painting.

"Can I pick cherries, Baka?"

"Get a bowl from the house and help yourself. But don't eat 'em till we wash them first." Then she reached up to one of the low, strong branches and plucked the reddest cherry I'd ever seen. "Pick low. Things ripen faster near the trunk."

While she hung clothes on the line nearby, I'd bring an old Birdseye Pudding container from her kitchen and shimmy back up the tree. I loved the sweet smell of the cherries and the feel of the smooth bark under my palms. When I got tired of picking, but wasn't ready to surrender my haven that let me look down to the rest of the world, I picked at the gray bark. The top layer wrapped around the branches like cellophane. If I were careful, I could peel away even strips. At first, I was only patient and steady enough to tear away enough to curl around my finger like a ring. As I got better, and luckier, I occasionally tore off enough to wrap around my wrist. I'd wear both the whole day through, emblems of my skill and success.

When Baka was done bringing in the wash, she'd help me rinse the cherries and remind me how to cut through them to check for worms. With her thumbnail, she'd split into even the thickest cherry, flick the pit into the colander in the sink, and rinse both halves of the cherry thoroughly before handing them to me.

"Don't eat too many," she'd warn, "you'll turn into a cherry tree." I'd eat those cherries all day, sometimes ripping them open like Baka showed me, sometimes just rubbing one under the tap so I could pop in the whole thing and shoot the pit from my mouth so hard it ricocheted around the sink.

I used to think Baka fed me so much lunch and dinner to fatten me up, but eventually I realized she was on a constant vigil to keep me from getting the cherry runs. Day and night, I ate them relentlessly. Even late into the evening, after she'd pulled out the hide-a-bed and a symphony of crickets forced us to turn up the television volume, I'd be eating those cherries.

"Here, have some popcorn," she'd hand me a freshly popped bowlful. "It's roughage." I'd alternate between a handful of popcorn and more cherries.

"Look," she snuggled next to me and held up my still-ornamented wrist and finger. "You are turning into a cherry tree."

When I was fourteen, my family joined the oil boom migration to Texas. It was no accident that the year we moved, Houston overtook Detroit as the fourth largest city in the U.S. I think the census shifted by an exact number—those that moved from the Motor City to the Bayou City.

I loved Texas immediately, but maintained contact with all my extended family still in Dearborn Heights and Hamtramck. Mostly I wrote to Baka.

"I have no trees to climb, Baka. There's nothing but huge pines all over our yard that shed prickly brown needles everywhere."

Trees seemed an unlikely topic for us to focus on, but trees it was, especially her cherry tree. At first Baka told me what I already knew about it: as one of the oldest trees on the block, it was bigger and fuller and prettier than anything in the neighborhood.

But then the news shifted to how the tree wasn't doing

so well. As I got older and busier, and we corresponded less frequently, the occasional news about the tree was always bad. She tried to save it by having a tree doctor do some special treatment that only accelerated its decline. By the time I graduated from high school, she said she'd had a good bit of it cut back as a last attempt to save it.

After a year in a college dorm, I moved into an apartment. The first letter I received at my own place began, "The cherry tree is dead. I had someone come to remove it, but he said that the trunk had to stay because the roots were so deep they couldn't be budged. So he cut it down to where the trunk divided into your four climbing branches." Though in my mind I'd claimed them years ago, I never knew she, too, thought of the branches as mine.

Not long after that letter, Baka died. With the cherry tree gone, she was having the outside of her house repainted by my cousin. One morning, he wondered why she didn't greet him with chrusciki and coffee as she usually did. Discovering an open window, he climbed in and found her dead from a midmorning heart attack that barely ruffled the sheets on her bed.

When my family returned for the funeral, we stayed at Baka's house. Before my father and I were set to leave my mother behind to sort through Baka's belongings, I slipped out to the backyard. Though everything else seemed smaller to me as an adult, the backyard felt huge and empty. There was so much sky I'd never seen from this yard before.

I approached my old cherry tree. Baka had arranged pots of fresh flowers between the severed branches. When I touched the trunk, I remembered the rings and wristbands I used to make from the bark. I tried to peel off a strip, but just a sliver

158

came free. I stuck it in my pocket and left.

Since college I've been a writer. "Write what you know," the books and professors always told me. It wasn't until I'd finished my third novel that I recognized a peculiar pattern: all my fiction is set in Michigan. Though I moved when I was only fourteen, rendering my experiences in Dearborn Heights a narrow slice of my entire life, each time I sit down to write what I know, I return home.

"Stay where the branches are sturdy and can support you," instructed Baka. "Pick low. Things ripen faster near the trunk."

"You'll turn into a cherry tree," she warned.

And finally she wrote, "The trunk has to stay because the roots are so deep."

My grandmother, wise woman.

Voices of Michigan

Uncle Earl's Princess

Linda LaRocque

To me, a visit from my Uncle Earl was equal only to Christmas. In fact, it was probably better.

He always drove a panel truck, an International panel truck, and with faded paint, rust and fenders flopping, he'd chug up our drive.

"Uncle Earl! Uncle Earl's here!" I knew the sound of that truck anywhere.

"Uncle Earl, Uncle Earl!"

Linda LaRocque is an award-winning playwright of more than five plays. Her most recent play, ***Revival at Possum Kingdom Community Church***, opened the 1999-2000 season of the Detroit Repertory Theatre. Several of her stories will be appearing in ***Chicken Soup for the Soul*** and ***Chicken Soup for the Unsinkable Soul***.

Shrieking, while running as fast as my scrawny legs would carry me, I'd run into the waiting arms of my most favorite person in the entire world.

"Spend the night, Uncle Earl! Stay for dinner! Stay forever!" I'd begin begging almost immediately. "Please, please. Promise you will."

"Hey, Princess." He called all the nieces that, but I didn't care, because I knew he "meant it" to me, and he was only being kind to the others. "I've got to go to Vermontville. Want to come along?"

Did I want to come along? I'd waited eternities for these magical moments.

"Ask your mother," he'd remind me.

Mother never cared.

"Just be back for supper, Earl," she'd call after us. "Would you please try to be on time -- for once? I hate holding dinner for you two."

He'd still be laughing when we'd pile into that old International.

"Did you remember a jacket, little girl?" It was mom again.

"Lil, she ain't no little girl. She's a princess today. If she gets chilly, she can wear one of my sweaters here. Quit worrying, will you? We'll be back in plenty of time."

Can you imagine? I was a princess! The old International was a coach. I was going off with my Uncle Earl. And I got to wear his sweater!

Life never could have dealt this poor little girl a better hand. I was jubilant. My cup runneth over -- even then.

"I'm cold, Uncle Earl."

"Well, grab that sweater. That's what they're for. You, Princess. They are for you."

I had to be in heaven or something. Seldom was I ever cold; I just said it because I wanted to wear his sweater.

So down the road we'd go. Just the two of us, talking, talking, and talking. He made me feel special and so important. I loved it.

The fact that I had a severe stutter mattered not to Uncle Earl. He loved me the way I was, and I knew it. He liked my company, and I knew that too.

Strange, how I can't remember a single thing we ever talked about. That didn't matter. What did matter was this man's kindness and compassion for a skinny kid with a stutter.

It's been a long time since those trips in the International. Uncle Earl is gone now. He was buried in The

Veterans' Cemetery on a rainy March afternoon. A simple service, with a handful of mourners and a cassette tape that played Taps in the background.

"Poor Earl died penniless," someone whispered. "Didn't leave a sorry thing to anybody."

Perhaps that's true, to some. But to me Uncle Earl left the greatest of legacies, a value system, that has enabled me to believe in myself -- because He believed in me first.

I realize now, he impacted my life more than anyone, and I like to think he continues to impact others as well. How so? By the lessons he taught me. You see, whenever I show kindness and compassion toward someone, it is due, I know, to those very seeds Uncle Earl sowed in me, by the accepting and caring way he lived his life. Thank you, Uncle Earl, wherever you are for all you have given me -- and by the way -- I'm still your princess.

Voices of Michigan

Knight Moves
How the Internet connected a father and his son

Brian Heeter

"Queen's Gambit. Ruy Lopez. Sicilian Defense. Castling." Words and terms from the past. I had grown up with them, not fully realizing exactly what they were. But more than twenty years later, I not only know what they are, but I use them almost nightly. It can all be traced back to genetics and the Internet.

Born and raised in Michigan, **Brian Heeter** is 29 years old. He lives in Grand Rapids with his wife, Kristi. **Brian** owns his own recruiting firm and works out of his home. He wrote an unpublished novel a few years ago, but now directs his writing toward short stories.

My father, Chris Heeter, loved chess. Studied it. Played it. Won trophies in chess tournaments. The first championship game I remember watching was the 1976 Super Bowl between Oakland and Minnesota. But years before, I could tell you that Bobby Fischer was the world champion in chess. I grew up surrounded by my dad's chess books. My favorite was *The World of Chess*. Inside the cover were pictures of chess sets from around the world. I was fascinated by the different styles and colors of the various pieces.

So how much did my father enjoy chess? He owned at least three chess sets. One was a very small travel set

165

that had holes in the squares and pegs on the pieces, so he could study moves while in a car. The second set was a more standard one with a beautiful carved board which folded up into a carrying case for the pieces. The pieces were classic Staunton style figures. Finally, there was a giant set, with over-sized pieces. It was really more of a showpiece than a gameboard.

There is a well-known story in my family about a Saturday when my dad had a friend over to play chess for the afternoon. My mom took my sister and me out for the day to give them a peaceful and quiet atmosphere in which to play. When she returned later that afternoon, my dad and his friend were gone. The chessboard, with pieces scattered about, lay on the table. She cleaned it up and began preparing dinner. Not much later, my dad and his friend returned to conclude their unfinished game. But the board was gone. Their jaws dropped and their hearts sank. Having stepped out to give themselves a break, they did not think about leaving a note requesting that the board be left alone. Their great struggle was never to be finished.

When I was six, my dad passed away. He never had a chance to teach me the game. Two years later, using a book from the library, I taught myself how to play chess. But I never had anyone to play against, no chance to hone any skill I might possess. Over the next twenty years, I played only a handful of games. I liked to play, but it became hard to find others who enjoyed the game. It was much easier to put together a pick-up basketball game or, in college, a quick game of euchre. Chess faded into the background. I did not think much about it.

166

Time moved on and so did I. Earlier this year, my wife and I purchased a new computer and merged onto the information superhighway. The Internet opened a whole new world. We could e-mail friends and family around the country and the world. We could download movie trailers. Working at home became much more productive. And then, one day, while surfing the Net, I discovered it. On-line chess. I decided to check it out.

It sounded like fun. I could play again. I worked my way through the site, and found an opponent. I settled in to play. Approximately six moves and two minutes later, the game was over. I lost, in an amazingly fast, horrible way. I stared at the screen. What the hell just happened?

I played another game. It lasted a little longer, but the ending was the same. I tried again. Another game, another loss. It was getting late. I had to work the next morning. But something in me snapped. I am Chris Heeter's son! I do not suck at chess. Chess is in my blood. I had to win before I went to bed. It was a quest, a long quest. It took a while, but it finally happened. A victory, earned on the board. The clock on the computer showed 4:00 AM. My pillow beckoned.

As I slept, it happened. I discovered I had inherited more than my physical looks from my father. A passion for chess sprung from within me. I began to play every night on-line. I played people around the world, opponents in Scotland, Mexico, and Canada. Frustrated at first, I slowly became better. I purchased a book on chess strategy and learned openings such as the King's Indian Attack, the Nimzo-Indian Defense, and the Queen's Gambit. I began to utilize the castling move. Wins became more frequent than losses. I started dreaming of chess moves at night.

But something even more important and dramatic happened. I felt a connection to my father, a bond that I had not felt in years. It had been twenty-two years since he passed away, and I would be lying if I said I had not thought of him every day. But as I grew older and started a life of my own, we seemed to have less and less in common. My looks and physical demeanor came from my father, along with certain personality traits such as my sense of humor and competitiveness. We both also lacked a certain *je ne sais quois*, or mechanical ability, as the French say. But the links stopped there. He was voted the "Hackett Heartthrob." I attended the same high school and certainly did not have the same effect on the ladies. He played tennis at Western Michigan. I played intramurel basketball at Michigan State. He never left Kalamazoo. I had a tour of duty in New Jersey, survived, and now reside in Grand Rapids.

Chess connects us. I understand why he loved the game so much. From what I can gather, he seemed to be a pretty good player. I think, over time, I can be. This game, with its strategy, moves, mystery, frustration, and glory, this is something we share.

It strikes as somewhat interesting that now, at 28, I am beginning to play. My father died when he was 28. Perhaps a torch has been handed over. If so, I will carry it proudly. Down the road, I hope to play in tournaments, and perhaps earn a trophy of my own. Until then, I will continue to perfect my game over the Internet, practicing perhaps with my father looking over my shoulder. And if heaven is how I imagine it, then one day I will be able to sit down to play the man from whom I inherited this passion. He will play white, and I will play black. I will look him in the eye, cock my left eyebrow (a trait from my mother), smile and say, "Your move."

Voices of Michigan

Remembrance

Shirley L. Dickman

It was always with reluctance that my mother let me visit Bonnie and Esley Lyles, my paternal grandparents. She had divorced their son, my father, when I was an infant, and any reminder of that part of her life was unwelcome to say the least. She said she liked Bonnie but found Esley a little "coarse." Nevertheless, she always permitted me to go, to my utter gratitude.

Shirley L. Dickman is enjoying retirement and the free time to pursue her hobbies: reading, writing, gardening, cooking and playing the piano. She always enjoyed writing and co-founded a writing support group called the "Scribblers," in Royal Oak, Michigan where she and her husband Richard have lived for forty years.

By the time I was in the fifth grade, after school Friday afternoons, I was allowed to catch the southbound Prospect bus which delivered me to the corner of Broadway and Prospect in downtown Kansas City. From there I'd walk the two blocks to my grandpa's used car lot. He'd usually be sitting with several of his cronies in the miniature, one-room house that served as the business office. The room was sparsely furnished - a fan in the summer, a portable heater in the winter, and grandpa's desk. In the center of the floor, there was a large, brass spittoon placed on old, yellow-stained sections of **The Kansas City Star**.

My arrival usually signaled time to lock up and head home, and as quickly as possible, for we always had big plans for Friday night. The drive home was colorful as Grandpa threaded his way in and out of the noisy, five o'clock traffic, continually laying on his horn and hollering at other drivers, "Get out of our way, you dirty dog," or "Speed it up, you slimy yellow-bellied s.o.b., me and Shirley are in a hurry." Finally, we'd arrive at the tall, three-story brick house that sat on a hill in the middle of the block on Spruce Street. Bonnie, in her apron, blue eyes twinkling, would be standing on the porch anxiously awaiting our arrival. After an enthusiastic round of hugs and kisses, we'd take our places at the big, old kitchen table where dinner, piping hot, would be waiting: crispy fried chicken with mashed potatoes and gravy, fresh green beans (with bacon fat), hot home-made biscuits with blackberry preserves, hot cinnamoned applesauce, and raisin or gooseberry pie, warm from the oven and topped with great scoops of vanilla ice cream.

Groaning from having overeaten, Grandpa and I would then leave Grandma to do the "women's work" and rush to the Grande Theater, hoping to arrive in time to get our favorite seats in the exact center of the tenth row from the stage. Usually, the organ recital would be underway, and we'd both be glad because that was our least favorite part of the program. Then, it would be time for the main event. The main event was a magic show or sometimes a juggler or acrobats and always a clown tossing hard candies into the audience. After the main event would come the movie. The movie, usually a western, would feature Gene Autry, Hopalong Cassidy, Red Ryder or Roy Rogers. It would be near midnight by the time we got home and then, very quietly, so as not to wake up Grandma, we'd prepare our midnight snack. Grandpa would slice bright yellow cheddar cheese into chunks and open the Armour Viennese Weiners, while I got out the Nabisco crackers from their yellow and red tin and brought in the ginger ale that was kept on the back porch. Then, we'd sit close together, whispering about the "best" parts of the movie and giggle when we heard Grandma snoring in the other room.

By the time bright rays of sun streaming through the lacy curtained window woke me up on Saturday morning, Grandma would have mown the lawn, carted the wicker basket full of Grandpa's freshly starched shirts to the backyard and hung them out to dry, prepared the evening meal and baked my favorite orange chiffon cake (with sixteen egg whites). While I'd dress and eat the breakfast she'd prepared, Grandma would shower, sprinkle her plump body with "scent of lavender," put on a crisp, flowered cotton house dress, and weather permitting be ready for the front porch.

The porch stretched the length of the house. The wooden floor (painted a glossy pine-green) next to the red brick of the house always reminded me of Christmas. Our "spot" was the huge porch swing (also painted green) that hung suspended from the ceiling. And that's where we'd idly chatter away the remainder of the hot Missouri afternoons, gently swinging and fanning ourselves and drinking frosty lemonade. I'd tell her about school and my piano lessons, and she'd always inquire about Katherine and Bill (my mother and stepfather), and my assorted sisters and brothers. Then, she would tell me about her youngest son, my Uncle Dillard, and his grocery business, and on rare occasions, drop a tiny clue as to the whereabouts of my mysterious father. (My father was an alcoholic, and apparently it had been decided that if I were never to make his acquaintance, it would be in my best interest. Of course, I knew nothing of this, and at the time was tremendously curious about this man of mystery.)

One time, Grandma's wrinkly, jolly blue eyes became uncommonly serious. She looked at me intensely, tiny beads of perspiration dampening her upper lip, and said, "Shirley, don't ever get around any I-talians. Over by the Katz Drugstore a car full of I-talians pulled a woman into their car and bit her breast right off." To this day that stands out in my memory as if seared into my brain by a branding iron.

Saturday evening meals were always more leisurely than the Friday night dinners. But at dinner Grandpa always did two things that I was pretty sure would fit my mother's idea of "coarseness." First was the prayer. Prayer was taken quite seriously in my home, so it always shocked me when, at Grandpa's, we would bow our heads and he would say, "Good bread, good meat, good God, let's eat!" And the second thing was he would never say, "Pass the potatoes, please," or "Pass the peas, please." He would simply point. If neither Grandma nor I happened to notice, he would *grunt* and point to whatever he wanted more of.

After dinner, Grandpa and I would ready the fire while Grandma cleaned up the kitchen. When the kitchen was sparkling and the fire was hissing and crackling, it would be time for the event of the evening, the Grand Old Opry. Grandpa would sit in his big reclining chair next to the smoking table and light his pipe. Grandma would sit in her rocker, and I'd lie on the soft, red patterned carpet next to the fire, enveloped in warmth. We all considered the "down-home" folks on the Grand Old Opry to be our old and cherished friends who had stopped in for the evening to visit; and, of course, the highlight of the visit would come when the announcer would finally say, "And now, ladies and gentlemen, from the heart of Nashville, into your living rooms, we are proud to bring you the one, the only...Cousin Minnie Pearl...."

"Howwwwwwwwwwwwdy! I'm mighty proud to be here!"

I'd always look at Grandpa who'd remind me of Santa Claus, with laughter shaking his body. He loved Cousin Minnie Pearl.

When the show was over we'd prepare for bed and the final ritual of our weekend together. Grandma would come out in her fluffy, flannel nightie, and Grandpa would noisily get settled in his sofa-turned-bed for the night in the adjacent room. Grandma and I would sink into our huge feather bed, cold sheets smelling of fresh air and smooth from having been ironed. Then, lights out...pin-drop silence...and, finally, from Grandpa's room, "Well, aren't we going to talk about the kin-folk?" Then it would start. There were Elmo and Alma and their "no count" sons; great grandma Lampton's cancer; Sam Lyles, Grandpa's third cousin once removed, and his grocery business; Aunt Golden's health (she was always poorly); there were Aubrey and Langley and on and on. And finally, the "trip to Versailles." It would start with, "Esley, we have to take Shirley down to the farm. She's never met Arthur and Wilma and Claudie and them, and then we'll go over to

Mattie and Charley Woolery's."

"Woman, are you crazy? Shirley, don't ever let this woman talk us into that trip. It would be the sorriest day of our life. They eat funny food down there. Their milk's got clumps, and their meat's in mason jars floatin' around in some liquid that looks like panther...."

"Esley!   Don't fill this child's head with such nonsense.   They're fine, Christian people and hard workers!"

"Bonnie, your Aunt Mattie Woolery is crazy as a coot, and everybody in Versailles knows that Charley Woolery is a hermit. No!! We're not draggin' Shirley down there and that's final!! End of conversation!!"

By now the big old clock in the living room would have gonged midnight, and feeling Grandma's plump body warmth next to me I'd sink down into the cloud-soft feather bed and drift off to sleep, still thinking about the kin-folk and wondering if we'd ever go to Versailles.

Lessons on the AuSable

Tom Derrickson

Sweat beaded on the old man's tanned, leathery forehead as he struggled to hold the 13 foot Grumman aluminum canoe steady in the current. The two-pronged, steel point on his long wooden canoe pole dug hard into the gravel bed of the AuSable River. Aided by a chain brake attached to a short rope dragging from the stern, he had stopped the canoe with quickness and precision. From my seat in the bow, I was in perfect position to present a dry fly toward the source of the rippling circles which were still expanding toward us from the run ahead.

Tom Derrickson is a private investigator, father of three and grandfather who lives in Muskegon, Michigan. He has attended both Michigan State and Grand Valley State Universities earning a B.S. in Legal Administration. This is his first attempt to write a story for publication.

I felt my heart pounding in anticipation of making a perfect cast to the rising trout. I drew my rod back with the orange fly line following obediently. It looped high and gracefully above and behind the canoe as I timed the forward thrust of my 7½ foot long fiberglass rod toward my target, excitedly expecting a perfect placement which would put yet another trout in my creel.

"Damn it, Tom, you hooked me in the ear again...Watch your back cast!"

"Sorry, Grandpa," I replied sheepishly.

177

The old man held the canoe steady with one hand while using the other to disengage the tiny #16 hook, adorned with black yarn, yellow chenille and rooster neck hackles, from the back of his ear. At the same time, he gently lectured me before throwing the imitation bumble bee back into the AuSable, slightly upstream and astern of the canoe, saying: "Try again, but this time be more careful."

The air was hot and still in Grayling at midday in late July. The deer flies and mosquitoes were biting more than the trout. Hours from now, an evening hatch would cause larger trout to begin feeding with reckless abandon after leaving their hiding places under the banks and brush piles. At this time of day, the trout tended to be smaller and more finicky. It would take a perfect presentation to coax this fish into taking a fly.

The coals from a 12" charcoal grill, heating in the center of the canoe for our shore lunch, only added to the heat that I felt as I anticipated my next cast. I wanted badly to catch this trout. It was holding in swift water near the end of a run, shaded by a large white pine leaning out over the river. I also wanted to avoid hooking my grandpa's ears or other appendages during my next back cast. My floating fly line was attached to a tapered lightweight monofilament leader which began to loop toward me in the current along the side of the canoe. I began stripping line into the bottom of the canoe.

Whether motivated by cowardice or quick thinking, I decided not to tempt fate twice by risking another back cast. I lifted my rod tip high and, with a powerful forward thrust, I executed a perfect roll cast above the run holding the feeding trout. The bumble bee impostor touched down softly on the water's surface as if landing to pollinate a flower. The fly drifted gently at first, but picked up speed as it entered the run. It accelerated toward the source of the expanding concentric rings which first caught our attention. The water erupted in an explosion of spray and foam as a 20" brown trout savagely attacked the drifting bee, using its large mouth to engulf what might be its last meal.

I brought my rod tip back sharply, setting the hook firmly in the upper jaw of the healthy trout which had spent its life growing strong in the cold, clear waters of the AuSable. My thin fly rod bent into an inverted U as the brown surged toward the brush on the far side of the river, seeking safety and possible freedom among the tangled roots and deep waters undercutting the far bank.

In my twelve years on this earth, I had faced similar battles on the Manistee, Pere Marquette, and Baldwin Rivers. Having lost many of them to logs, current, and strong, smart trout, I knew that I must test the strength of my thin 6X leader by turning this heavy fish. The odds were not in my favor. Fortunately, the brown surged upstream so that I would not also have to battle the weight of the current. In fact, I would use the force of the current as my ally.

My line started to sing as it drew taut against the surging fish. The brown darted toward the submerged branches of an over-hanging tag alder. I had no choice but to increase the pressure. I used all of the flex and backbone of my fly rod to distribute and counteract the force created by the running trout. Something had to give. If the brown failed to turn or wrapped my line around the submerged brush, the battle would soon be over. In a stroke of pure luck, which sometimes befriends fishermen and young children, the trout turned just before reaching its safe haven and swam back into a deeper, more tranquil, pool next to the canoe. Being within seconds of leader separation or the hazards near the far bank, which would have brought freedom, the trout's unexpected turn evened the odds.

The brown then broke water in a somewhat uncharacteristic tactic for its species and surged skyward, shaking and turning, in an effort to dislodge the hook. It re-entered the water with a loud splash. After what seemed an eternity, I worked the brown toward the edge of the canoe. My rod tip pounded into the water as the brown tried valiantly to escape with some last pumps and surges. I eased the fish toward Grandpa, who now held his landing net at the water's surface. He gently eased the net under and around the fish just as the fly pulled loose. This beautiful trout was now mine.

I looked with great pride at this large brown, admiring its thickness and orangish-brown, glistening sides. The dark red and black spots surrounded by white with bluish hues were indicators that this fish had spent its entire life in the river. It did not have the characteristic orange spots of a planter. The pride in the old man's eyes was directed toward me, reflecting the satisfaction of a teacher in confirming that his pupil is starting to catch on. But my lesson was not yet over.

"What should we do with this fish?" grandpa queried. The question made me feel uncomfortable. The old man pointed to several smaller trout already resting on a bed of wet grass in my creel, which were clearly better table fare.

"This brown gave you a good fight. We'll catch more down river for tomorrow's fish fry. Why not release it to spawn so you can come back every year to catch more browns?" I was being given a choice, not a command, unlike last season when Grandpa made me release two 23" and 25" small mouth bass, the biggest I had ever caught or seen, after catching them one day before the season opener. At first, I was appalled by the thought of releasing this fish. I had caught larger browns, but not on a fly rod with such light line. I caught this fish in a fair battle and it was mine. Why should I release it? It wasn't fair.

Grandpa looked intently at me while awaiting a response, with nothing in his demeanor which would suggest that his approval was contingent upon my decision. I didn't feel pressured. I knew that my decision would be accepted without comment or argument and that our fishing would continue uninterrupted by lectures or hard feelings.

Reluctantly, and a bit sadly, I agreed that releasing the fish would be a good thing. At the old man's instruction, I wet both of my hands to protect the trout's skin before firmly but gently grasping it around its thick girth. I then cradled the brown along side of the canoe and lowered it into the water, headfirst into the current, forcing oxygenated water through its gills. The brown revived quickly and, with a muscular wriggle, slipped from my hands and headed rapidly to the quiet safety awaiting it under the far bank. Up until the final moment of separation, I struggled silently with my decision. When the fish was gone, I felt bad…and good, at the same time. It would be years before I knew why.

The trip continued downstream in the company of beavers, white tailed deer, ducks, and snapping turtles. The canoe glided effortlessly over tall, submerged aquatic grasses which provided a home for small trout and the larval stages of some of the insects that fed them. Occasionally a pat, or ruffed grouse, drummed its wings in the distance or exploded from the riverbank in a heart-stopping explosion of sound.

The promise of adventure loomed around each bend as Grandpa pointed out corduroy roads and the remnants of long-abandoned logging camps and towns. Each site had a story and Grandpa's knowledge of local history was impressive. An occasional white pine, which had escaped the logger's ax in the 19th century, stood in the forest as a silent testimony to a Michigan landscape which had been covered with these giant trees, blanketing the forest floor in perpetual shade.

Hardwoods had now become the dominant forest species. Non-native brown and rainbow trout had replaced the now extinct grayling and increasingly rare brook trout as the dominant AuSable fish. Occasionally, we hooked and landed a native brook trout. There is nothing in God's creation more beautiful or tasty than a freshly-caught, native-Michigan, brook trout.

I was lucky to have a grandfather who was both a fishing guide and local historian. He was once featured in a television special on the popular Thursday night **Michigan Out of Doors** program, guiding Mort Neff's staff on a fishing trip down "our" river. I never ceased to marvel at Grandpa's ability to maneuver a canoe downstream with a pole while simultaneously fly-fishing from the stern and telling stories. It is a skill I studied and tried unsuccessfully to master, as did many others. He could cast his fly with the precision of a surgeon which was his former profession before finding his true calling as a fly fisherman.

Shore lunch was something to which we both looked

forward. The cooking aroma of flame-broiled hamburgers, freshly caught trout, fried potatoes and onions mingled with the scent of pine and a sweet organic fragrance which permeated the clear northern Michigan air. The tensions of life were temporarily put aside, yielding to the serenity of Grayling's woods, the beautiful AuSable, and the pleasure of the moment. It was a quiet time to talk about things of mutual interest as water skippers skated and danced across the surface of the water along the bank. A background chorus of frogs, birds, and insects produced a unique and unmistakable northern Michigan sound.

Elsewhere in the world, the cold war was raging and people were building bomb shelters. The Cuban missile crisis was looming on the horizon, and it would frighten us all before year's end. Yet, all was well and at peace on the AuSable.

Grandpa and I found common denominators during our shore lunch conversations to span the years between us. Baseball was one of them. Grandpa had played on the 1918 VanBuren County Championship baseball team, in an age before television, when communities had their own teams which competed during the lazy days of summer. We discussed how the Yankees won too much and how the Tigers had a poor chance of winning the 1962 pennant. When the Tigers finally won the World Series in 1968, and again in 1984, I thought of my grandfather.

After shore lunch, we packed up all of our garbage and tied it to the inside of the canoe. We often picked up messes left by others to preserve this pristine habitat in an era when environmental stewardship was in its infancy. We caught and lost more browns and rainbows as we continued downstream.

We released some and kept others for our long-anticipated family fish fry. When I "caught a squirrel" by hooking my fly in the brush with an errant back cast, Grandpa deftly used the prongs on the end of his pole to capture, twist, and snap off the branch to which the fly was attached for a quick recovery of the expensive fly.

As we rounded a bend near journey's end, we encountered a bait fisherman directly in our path. Unlike me, Grandpa disliked bait fishing for trout, which he considered to be an unsportsman-like pursuit engaged in by "meat fishermen." I took care never to talk to Grandpa about the large brown trout I frequently caught and kept when fishing with live nightcrawlers after dark. Grandpa knew that I bait fished for trout, and I knew that he disapproved of the practice. I figured that he tolerated this knowledge because he saw some promise in converting me to a full time fly fisherman, while patiently cutting me some slack due the ignorance of my youth.

Grandpa didn't know, and never was told, how I had secretly taught his older brother (my great uncle Albert) to enjoy bait fishing for trout. Uncle Albert, publicly at least, was also an avowed fly-fishing purist. I found it flattering (and unusual) that an elderly, well-educated, and still practicing physician would want a 12-year-old boy to teach him anything. This clandestine instruction took place at my uncle's request because of my already established reputation as a successful bait fisherman. Uncle Albert was perhaps the nicest man I ever met and also a quick learner when it came to bait fishing. I had to assure him that I would not tell Grandpa about this bait fishing business because "Ralph would cut my ears off" if he ever knew. It was a secret that I kept for Uncle Albert until both he and Grandpa Ralph were gone.

With these thoughts in mind, I wondered how Grandpa would react to this bait fisherman, blocking the path of his canoe, who threatened the trout fishing philosophy which he held so sacred. Grandpa hit the brakes hard with his canoe pole, just before reaching the bait fisherman. He then stared intently at this man who was standing waist deep in the river, separating the current like a large rock.

The bait fisherman raised his rod tip high, poised to cast a fat nightcrawler into the sacred waters of the AuSable. He stopped his cast and glanced quizzically at the old man stopped in the canoe near him. That dangling night crawler must have assumed the proportions of an anaconda in my grandfather's eyes as he continued to stare at it. Surely, Grandpa would not let this heresy go unchallenged without some remark. After a short but seemingly infinite silence, the remark came.

"On which side do you want to be passed, sir?" Grandpa politely inquired. The fisherman looked incredulously at the old man and said: "I'll be damned; you are the first SOB in a canoe all day who has cared enough to ask that question." As we passed quietly and carefully behind the bait fisherman so as not to spook the fish in the area, Grandpa wished him good fishing.

By mid-afternoon, we reached the pull out point where Grandma had spotted Grandpa's old fishing car, a vintage vehicle used solely for this purpose. After we loaded the canoe, Grandpa drove slowly along narrow two tracks, while overhanging branches scratched the sides of his fishing car. Upon reaching a paved road, Grandpa pulled over to the shoulder and took a homemade butterfly net from the trunk. He told me to hold it out of the window and into the roadside grass as he drove slowly along the shoulder of the road. The net cut through the tall dry grasses, scooping up grasshoppers by the dozens. Every few hundred yards we would stop, shake out the bees and grab the grasshoppers to put in a homemade container made of wood, tire tubing, and window screen. The grasshoppers would spit disgusting "tobacco juice" all over us as we grabbed them.

Once caught, the grasshoppers became bait for use in catching hand sized bluegills on Lake Margrethe, west of Grayling, where Grandpa lived during the non-winter months. His winters were spent plying the waters of Lake Powell in Arizona or fly fishing for bonefish in the shallow salt-water flats off the Florida Coast.

Grandpa never saw an inconsistency in using live bait for lake fishing while spurning the practice for trout. Trout were accorded a higher status than lake-dwelling fish and were, therefore, treated differently. Ironically, Grandpa's 16-foot green fiberglass pole used to catch bluegills was affectionately named "the meat getter." True to form, however, he released large female bluegills to repopulate the lake for future generations. That evening, fishing from a 12-foot boat with an ancient Johnson motor, we caught a large wire basket full of bluegills, which seemed to find the grasshoppers irresistible. A few small mouth bass also succumbed to the temptation of this gourmet offering.

As we fished for bluegills, Grandpa and I cast a couple of pike rods over the opposite side of the boat. Large red and white bobbers, attached to heavy line with a wire leader and a giant hook, were suspended over and along the nearby weed bed. The 4-6" minnows we used for bait had been captured earlier in another fishing opportunity. Grandpa paid me ten cents for each shiner and five cents for each chub that I caught from the dock in front of his cottage.

Casting the minnows drew the attention of seagulls and Grandpa cautioned that I should cast away from them. When I cast my shiner too close to a low flying gull, it dove into the water and grabbed my sinking shiner before I could pull it away. My line became entangled with the seagull, which burst from the water to attempt an airborne escape. I'll never forget the strange sensation of fighting a seagull on a pike rod as it flew up and around me, pumping the rod like a fish.

I reeled in the distraught bird to be untangled by Grandpa, who by now had donned a leather glove. We released the bird unharmed, but I suspect that it thought twice about looking for future meals around boats. I received a patient reprimand about how the incident could have been avoided, just as I had when I lost two of grandpas anchors to the depths of Lake Margrethe for failing to tie them on properly. Errors in life, like baseball, were part of the game, which provided opportunities for instruction rather than punishment.

We boated two 30" northern pike in addition to the other fish. These toothy giants have a firm and delicious white flesh if one can tolerate the challenge of picking tiny Y-bones from between one's teeth. We returned to the cottage with a bright orange sunset falling into the lake at our backs.

After helping to clean the fish, I turned in early and slept soundly, breathing the cool northern Michigan air coming through the bedroom window. I was lulled to sleep by

187

the sound of gentle waves lapping onto the beach outside of my window and the tic toc...tic toc sound that came from the swinging pendulum of the grandfather clock just outside of my open bedroom door.

I awoke at sunrise to the smell of Grandma's scrambled eggs prepared with dried northern Michigan morel mushrooms. After breakfast, Grandpa loaded the grandkids and cousins into boats for an early morning seashell hunt along the shores of Lake Margrethe. He knew of a secret beach where they could be found. It never occurred to us as youngsters that sand dollars, conch shells, nautilus and abalone were not native to northern Michigan lake shores. The older ones were a little suspicious, but their concerns faded quickly as they scrambled for the treasures which were scattered over a large section of white beach. Grandpa spent months during the winter combing the beaches in Florida to collect these Gulf and Atlantic seashells in anticipation of shell hunting in Michigan with his grandchildren.

The late afternoon fish fry was a lakeside social event for relatives and occasional guests who dropped by. One of Grandpa's fishing buddies was Fred Bear. To me, this archery legend was a gentle giant with large hands who just happened to enjoy hunting tigers and Kodiak bears with a bow and arrow. Another occasional summer neighbor was Ann Marsten, female National Archery Champion and Miss Michigan. Perhaps only in Michigan could a female archer use archery as her talent in winning the Miss Michigan Pageant at a time when beauty pageants were just that. I knew that she must be special when I frequently saw her display her archery skills on my favorite show from early childhood, **Captain Kangaroo**.

188

Grandpa was always the designated fish fryer. I still have visions of him dipping the fish in his special batter before carefully sprinkling salt and pepper on each fish, inside and out. The fish were fried in hot oil until golden brown in a row of electric frying pans sitting atop card tables under poplar trees next to the lake. The leaves from the poplar trees rustled constantly in the afternoon breeze creating a sound more beautiful than that produced by the finest wind chimes. Frog legs and snapping turtles were also offered as unique Michigan delicacies. Although the thought of them brought mixed reviews, they were truly delicious.

Locally grown and freshly-picked produce was added to the feast. For dessert, we enjoyed wild blueberry pie, carefully picked by the grandkids and cousins at Grandpa's secret wild blueberry patches. Our Brittany Spaniel, Duffy, also participated in the blueberry picking expeditions by lying down with a blueberry bush between his paws, picking it clean with his teeth and tongue.

As I grew older, I had less time to fish with Grandpa. As happens with many teenagers, dreams of girls and cars began to replace my lust for trout. I continued tying my own trout flies and Grandpa became my field tester, candidly critiquing my successes and failures, in terms of construction quality, artistry and fish appeal. Correspondence replaced personal contact, but I looked forward to those exchanges. Some of my insect creations proved to be winners, so I supplied extra flies to outfit Grandpa and some of his fishing buddies.

The years passed quickly. I became a father and a grandfather. I shall always remember the summers of fishing and fun in Michigan's northern woods. The lessons of patience, courtesy, tolerance, conservation and a loving respect for Michigan's great outdoors were deeply implanted into my being. The legacy of my grandfather is more than a faded sign located on the northeast shore of Lake Margrethe that identifies VanVleck Park. The park was named in Grandpa's honor for his efforts to preserve and protect the unique northern Michigan environment while educating others about its history.

To this day, for strange, unknown reasons, the great grandchildren of Dr. Ralph VanVleck are still finding sand dollars, conch shells, nautilus and abalone on Lake Margrethe and other northern Michigan lakes. Fish are still being caught with some reaching the dinner table while others are released to perpetuate the species. Tales of adventure from Michigan's past echo through the forest in the company of beavers, white tailed deer, ducks, snapping turtles and an occasional drumming ruffed grouse. A chorus of frogs, birds, and insects in the forest continues to sing, accompanied by the rustling leaves of poplar trees. The water skippers still dance and skate along the water's edges of the AuSable to the great delight of those who have the good fortune to experience northern Michigan.

Farewell

Linda Barlekamp

I'm giving part of me away today. I am not doing it of my own accord. My parents feel that our dog is too big for our small house. They say there are too many people in the house for a big dog, and Mom is going to have another baby. Princess does take up a lot of space. She always seems underfoot. Seven people now live in the house: my parents, my brother, two sisters, me, my grandmother--and this one on the way will make eight. I really want to keep Princess but my parents feel it is terrible to confine a large dog just to the basement, and they are probably right. Rusty gold, almost the height of an Irish setter, but broader, Princess fools everyone--she is really a pedigree cocker spaniel. From the expression on my parents' faces when she arrived, I guess cocker spaniels are different in Europe than in America.

About five years ago Princess arrived from Belgium, a special gift from our aunt and uncle, especially for us kids. A truck delivered her on the Sunday before Christmas. We were in the middle of everything: the bulbs, lights, tinsel, and needles--it was tree decorating time! The truck pulled to a stop in front of the house. Confusion and noise suddenly broke out because we realized it was coming to our house.

Linda Barlekamp lives in Kentwood, Michigan with her husband, Bob, and two children, Christopher and Courtney. She is a reading specialist at Robinson Elementary in Grand Haven, Michigan.

191

Princess, as we had already named her, was hunched over in her cage. No one had any idea she would be so big! Crowding around the cage in excitement, we tried to coax her out. Finding she couldn't cringe back any further into the cage and tempted by the open door after such a long confinement, she finally ventured into the cluttered, noisy living room where we kids instantly tried to hug her. She fled under the coffee table.

In two years, she was so big that to crawl under the table meant she would knock it over. Of course, she only tried to hide there when she did something wrong, like the time she stole the pot roast from the kitchen table when my grandmother's back was turned or when she chewed up my younger sister's baby shoe or the time she ate a pair of my glasses--including most of the glass! I remember the time she ran out of the open backyard gate and was hit by a car just down the block. We were scared to death--and so was she. Mom and Mrs. Woods, our next door neighbor, carried her home--the big lug wasn't hurt, but she stayed under the table all afternoon.

As she grew older, and I became a teenager, she spent more time in the basement. I loved to join her there--to pet her and to tell her my problems. She listened and licked my hands. She became "my" dog. To be with her in the basement meant I could escape from the noise and the people upstairs. Like any teenager, I was searching for a little space-- a place for myself. Princess didn't care if I talked or cried. She just listened, head in my lap. Maybe she needed a little space, too.

I'll always remember today....

It isn't noisy. Everyone is gone. I am sitting on the cold, cement porch steps with Princess, waiting, waiting for Mrs. Thomas to pick us up. She's a distant friend of the family, and she is taking Princess and me to her house. Mrs. Thomas's brother and niece are waiting there, and I'm supposed to hand Princess over to them. Mrs. Thomas is going to give us one of her dog's puppies; she has a toy poodle.

Glancing at my watch, I realize Mrs. Thomas should have been here 15 minutes ago. "Maybe she forgot," I pray.

Watching a car slow to a stop in front of the house. I knew my prayer wasn't being answered. Standing up, Princess and I slowly walk down the sidewalk to the blue Pontiac. She leaps into the car (Princess loves car rides), and I climb in the back seat next to her.

"I hope you weren't waiting for me very long. I got out of the hairdresser's a little later than I thought I would," Mrs. Thomas said.

"No, I haven't been waiting long," I answer quietly.

"I am sorry. My brother and niece must be waiting, too. I know my niece, Karen, is just going to love the dog," Mrs. Thomas said, trying to strike up a conversation. "Her name is Princess, isn't it?"

"Yes," I reply.

"How long have you had her?"

"About five years now." I just wish she'd stop talking; my stomach is in knots.

"I hope you will like your new dog when you get her."

"I hope I will, too." I answer vaguely. I feel terrible. I don't want a new dog. I don't want to give Princess up-- she's mine. I can't just walk over to Mrs. Thomas's niece and hand her the leash and say, "Here she is. I'm sorry you had to wait so long." Her niece can wait forever.

The car is stopping. We are at her house. Walking up the sidewalk, I tighten my grip on Princess's leash--and my emotions. Entering the house slowly, I greet Mr. Thomas, and he introduces me to the father and daughter who are taking away my dog.

I try to talk to the girl, restraining my tears as my hand strokes the gold velvet coat of my dog lying at my feet. I have to make sure this stranger will take special care of her.

They're standing up to leave, and I guess I'm expected to walk Princess out to their car. Holding the dog's leash tightly, I open the car door. Princess jumps in eagerly, as always; then, she looks at me as if to ask why I'm not getting in, too. With my eyes full of tears, I struggle to unlock the leash. I gently stroke her head. I scratch behind her long, silky ears. (She always likes that.)

I shut the car door as Karen and her dad climb into the front seat. I follow Mr. and Mrs. Thomas back into the house, barely able to contain the tears that flow inside. Mrs. Thomas is saying something, but I ignore it, and I turn away so she can't see me. As I turn, I sense something moving to the right of me. From a box hidden in the corner, Mrs. Thomas lifts out a little, white ball of fur. I barely hear her say, "I want to show you your new dog."

"What?" I ask, not really comprehending.

"This is your dog," she repeats, holding the puppy out so that I can see it.

Inside, I'm screaming, *No, it's not...my dog just left! That's not mine! You can keep it!*

Standing silently for a moment, barely swallowing, I somehow manage to say, "I'm going home now...no, you don't have to drive me...it's not far and I'd rather walk. Thanks a lot...."

Instead of reaching for the dog, I reach for the doorknob, knowing I have to get out of there before I cry. Crying has to wait until I get home. Nobody will be there now. Even the basement will be empty....

Voices of Michigan

Ironwood in Wartime:
An Excerpt from "'Up North': A Family Memoir"

Robert L. Trezise

When we moved from the old house on McLeod Avenue to Sutherland Street in 1942, the war was on and Ironwood, located on the westernmost end of Michigan's Upper Peninsula, was a different place. I was ten years old.

Downtown had always been a bustling, congested place, and at night it was bright with neon signs of all sizes, the largest one being the glittering "Ironwood" sign that hung over the marquee of the magnificent Ironwood Theatre in the middle of Aurora Street. Now, the downtown was dark at night-- there was not a single neon display, and even the bright lights of the theatre marquee were turned off. There was not a single light in any of the shop windows.

Robert L. Trezise grew up in Ironwood, Michigan, attended Northwestern University and Michigan State, earned his Ph.D in 1966, taught school for several years and has had many articles published in professional education journals. He supervised teacher certification in the Michigan Department of Education until his retirement in 1991. He and his wife currently spend time in Lansing as well as Kewadin, Michigan.

Before the war on Saturday nights, when all the stores stayed open, half the town would go downtown and walk up and down the busy streets. Many people, like the Tomkins from church, would find a place to park on Aurora Street

197

early in the evening, as dressed up as they'd be on a Sunday morning (no lady would think of going downtown without her hat and gloves on), and they'd sit there the whole evening, watching all the people strolling past the brightly lighted windows, often cluck-clucking over the rowdy boys who stood around and made comments to the girls. But it was dead downtown on Saturday nights now. The boys were all gone.

One day I heard Dad say that some towns were beginning to encourage their stores to stay open Friday nights, rather than Saturdays--apparently as a part of the war effort; and soon the stores in Ironwood began to do that. It was strange, almost unthinkable, not to have the stores open Saturday nights.

People at home were told not to burn lights needlessly, and Mr. Hendricks, the school principal, told us that we should tell our parents to keep the window shades drawn halfway during the day to save on heat, and drawn all the way at night, not only to save on heat, but also make the town a less visible target for possible Japanese bombers.

For with the iron mines, we were told that Ironwood was considered a prime target. The Japanese—referred to as "Japs" in those days—could fly something called "the great circle route" right over the North Pole and bomb us any time. In order to warn us if such a thing happened, a forty-foot watch tower was built on top of Mt. Zion, and volunteers were solicited to keep watch up there.

Dad joined the effort and was assigned the 9:00 to 11:00 shift every other Wednesday night. I remember going up there with him one very stormy Wednesday, the night before Thanksgiving, when the snow made it difficult to get up Mt. Zion in a car. So the police came and took Dad and me up the treacherous Mt. Zion road in a police car which had chains on the tires. Riding in a police car was quite an adventure.

I can remember sitting in the little room at the top of the tower, watching the snow blow around the windows and listening to the wind howl.

We sat there quietly--listening for enemy planes.

Tuesdays were Bond days in school when all the students got to buy defense stamps. I bought one ten-cent stamp every Tuesday. But I was envious of Ruth Peterson, who always bought ten stamps. Ruth's father was a minister and was serving as a chaplain in the South Pacific. The teacher always praised Ruth for buying so many stamps. But Dad said I couldn't buy that many because he bought defense bonds at work.

Gas was rationed, but people who needed to have cars for "the war effort" had "A" cards which allowed them to buy more gas. We had only a "B" card, so we did very little driving for pleasure. Once, though, we drove out to Little Girl's Point at Lake Superior on a Sunday afternoon. Before the war, the park was always crowded with picnickers on Sundays, and the wonderful aroma of grilling meat hung heavy in the air. But now the place was desolate. The grass had grown long, and the big log pavilion, built by the C.C.C. boys, was boarded up. Even the rest rooms, built out of Lake Superior stones, were padlocked shut. The scores of picnic tables that once held lavish spreads of food were piled over near the edge of the woods. There was a bleakness and sadness about the place.

What a difference the war made.

Skirts got really short--to save on material. Even

making an allowance for the war effort, though, Mother and Aunt Mary thought Geraldine's skirts were shorter than they needed to be. Geraldine, my cousin, lived down the street from us and was a telephone operator.

Many of the movies were patriotic war stories. Everyone in the theatre would cheer when an enemy plane was shot down. But I always wondered what those last moments were like for the pilot--even if he was the enemy--as his plane plunged into the sea.

Families put red service banners with stars on them in their windows—one blue star if one boy in the family was in the service, two for two boys, and so on. One flag up in the Aurora Location had five stars. Mother didn't want a banner in our window, showing my brother, Arthur, was in the service--she wasn't into that kind of patriotic display. But I put one up anyway. I was proud that my big brother was a soldier.

In church the usually jovial Li'l Tregembo looked grim up there in the choir loft, especially on the Sunday when the news from Iwo Jima was so bad. That's where her son Sam was. I remember the Sunday morning Mrs. Warner came back to church after her son was reported killed in action. She came back too soon, because as soon as the first hymn started, "All Hail the Power of Jesus' Name"--the wonderful Diadem version, which was a great favorite with our largely Cornish congregation, she fled the sanctuary, sobbing loudly, dampening the fervor of the singing.

The Daily Globe frequently reported boys "missing in action" or "killed." The dreaded telegram from the war department always began with the same words: "We regret to inform you...."

Mother read Ernie Pyle in the Duluth News Tribune every morning. Pyle was famous for his descriptions of everyday G.I. life at the front lines. But Pyle was killed by a Japanese sniper toward the end of the war. Mother's eyes filled with tears when she heard the news on the radio.

Once in the late fall we went to Uncle Joe's cottage at Lake Gogebic for a few days, and one cold night Mr. and Mrs. Thacker, wrapped in heavy coats, rowed over from Merriweather in their canoe to visit us.

Mrs. Thacker ran a fashionable dress shop in downtown Ironwood that specialized in fitting women with corsets. Mr. Thacker--Ernie--was famous for being an expert on the war and had big maps of the war zones on his walls in his house. He said he kept pins of various colors in the maps to keep track of where all the big troop movements were occurring.

That night, as we sat around the hot fire in the big iron stove, Mr. Thacker talked with authority about how, when, and where the war would end. He sounded almost like a general. Later, when we saw them off at the dock, and they paddled silently away into the darkness, Mother said, "Well, Ernie always knows all the answers."

Another evening Herb and Esther Matthews stopped by. Herb was Aunt Lizzie's son–Grandma Eddy's nephew. Mr. Matthews said that one of the young men in his family, the organist in the big Methodist church up in Ely, had been in the Navy, but was discharged--and was now having mental problems as a result of a war experience.

One night the ship he was on in the South Pacific sank a Japanese destroyer; after the ship went down, the American ship ran down the Japanese survivors as they struggled in the black water. It was a brutal scene, Mr. Matthews said, and the young Matthews could not get the screams of the Japanese sailors out of his mind.

Arthur, Jr., whom everyone called "Junior," was going to junior college in Ironwood when his draft notice came. He had to go to Marquette for his physical. There was a lot of doubt he would pass it, though, because he was so nearsighted.

Mother, Dad, my sister, Mary Elizabeth, and I were sitting in the living room the night he came back from his physical. I'll never forget it. He bounded in the front door, shouting "Yippee! Yippee!" at the top of his voice, and he threw his hat in the air. "I passed! I passed!" and he took Mother in his arms and danced around the room.

Later he took some tests and scored exceptionally high on them, so he was put in a special program, called A.S.T.P., designed to train soldiers in high-level technical skills.

First he went to Ashland, Wisconsin, to study, and then to Chicago. During that time, he wrote to us about a new thing they were using in the military called "radar," which he was studying. After a period of study there, he took his basic training at Fort Benning. But before his basic training was completed, the A.S.T.P program was terminated by Congress. Later he was stationed in various camps in Georgia, Louisiana, and California. On September 21, 1944, Dad got a telegram from him in Camp Cooke. "I'm finally getting my furlough. Please send fifty dollars."

In a week or so, he came home.

In spite of the gas rationing, we took several little trips during the week that Junior was home.

One day in school, Mrs. Erickson, my eighth grade

teacher, asked me to stay after school so she could help me with the concept of ratio, which we were studying in arithmetic. I couldn't seem to get it when it was explained in class. But Mrs. Erickson was a patient teacher, and once again, after school, she explained how ratio worked. I finally said I got it, but I didn't. I didn't consider myself very smart--certainly not in arithmetic. And certainly not like my brother.

Anyway, when I got home from school, everyone was at the door waiting for me. It was a brilliant fall day, and the leaves were in full color. Mother said they had decided to take a little trip to Bayfield, a quaint little fishing village beyond Ashland on Lake Superior.

When we got there, it was late afternoon, but still warm and sunny. We took the little excursion boat to Madelaine Island, and we also visited the apple orchards around the village, where the workers--mainly older men--were in the process of harvesting the fruit.

But the little village, usually busy with tourists, was, like almost everything else those days, nearly deserted; there was a melancholy feeling about the place, in spite of the late-afternoon, golden sunshine. Also, we knew that Junior's furlough soon would be over, and he probably would be going overseas.

The next day--Junior's last day of the furlough--he stuck around the house. "That day he was strangely quiet," Dad was later to say. "He hardly left my side." That was the day, too, he took me aside and solemnly asked me to call him "Arthur," not "Junior," which I somehow found a little embarrassing.

He left on the 6:30 Chicago Northwestern train in the evening. Mother became almost hysterical on the depot platform. She clung to him, sobbing. Arthur could hardly break away to get on the train.

The scene made Mary Elizabeth and me uncomfortable, and we started back for the car. I glanced around to see if anyone was looking. But the people near by looked only sympathetic. Tearful farewells on train platforms were not unusual in those days. Arthur reported for duty at Camp Luis Obispo, where he stayed until February, 1945, when he was shipped to France--landing at LaHavre.

At that point, the war in Europe was drawing to a close. Arthur trekked across France and Germany as a part of the final clean-up of the German soldiers.

His letters home were filled with his usual zest and humor. He told us about how, during the breaks in their marches, he would practice his creeping and crawling, just because he liked to creep and crawl--but also because creeping and crawling while everyone else was resting appealed to his sense of clowning around to make everyone laugh. During the long marches, he passed time by imagining he was walking in Ironwood. In a letter he wrote, "In my mind I am walking from our front porch down Ayer Street and down to work at the A&P, taking note of all the things I pass. When I walk in the door and say hello to Frank Boho, I know ten minutes have passed."

He also passed time on the marches by solving mathematical problems in his head. "Last night, as we marched along through the dark, I worked for a while on a binomial expansion of (a plus b) to the 10th power. I finished it too."

On May 16, when he turned twenty, he was in Mannheim, where life suddenly turned quiet. Germany had surrendered unconditionally. Mother's box of cousin jack cookies arrived the day after his birthday, but, he wrote on the 17th, "Aunt Carrie guessed it just right. Her card arrived yesterday--right on the big day."

He continues in that same letter: "We've been leading the good life here. Beautiful sunny days, which follow with such regularity that I almost forget to appreciate them. The army makes few intrusions into our leisure."

German civilians did many of their chores. "They've washed our clothes, swept our rooms, fixed our beds, eaten leftovers from our field rations, and heated water for our coffee. I've heard a lot about treachery on their parts, but I haven't seen any of it myself. Except when you ask them if there are any Deutshen Soldater in their homes, they invariably say there are none--but sometimes there are. But they're always very peaceful, weary young guys, whom we rouse out of their beds. We ask them if they have any weapons, and they always say no to that, too. But sometimes they do. That's the extent of the German treachery."

In spite of the language problem, Junior talked as best he could to an old German. "The old man asked me about his beloved Augsburg and Munchen. When I told him about the devastation we saw there, he smote his brow in Biblical anguish, and while I'm not sorry our bombing has been effective, I hate the fact that war can happen to anyone--even Germans.

A day or so later he wrote another letter--an ominous one. "One day in Matsee there was a funeral, a real European funeral with a black coffin being carried down the street while ranks of women followed, their folded hands entwining their rosaries. Meantime, penetrating every corner of the village, the bell from the cathedral solemnly tolled. I thought of John Donne's sermon: '...each man is a piece of the continent, a part of the whole--and, therefore, send not to find for whom the bell tolls. It tolls for thee.'"

On Monday, March 28, Junior wrote his last letter ever. "The outgoing mail leaves this afternoon. We aren't leaving Mannheim for a few days, though. Maybe my next chance to write will be from France. Yes--we are practically on our way home. No foolin'."

The letter ends: "Don't expect any mail from me for at least a week."

The next day, Junior was apparently sitting on his bunk, while someone nearby was examining a German rifle he had recently found on a sightseeing tour of Hitler's den near Berchtesgaden. The rifle went off, striking Arthur in the head, killing him instantly.

We, of course, in Ironwood, remained oblivious to the tragedy. We only knew that Junior's Blackhawk Division was, according to the papers, on its way home and, in fact, had landed in New York.

One evening Mother mentioned at dinner that Major Bong, the air ace from Superior, Wisconsin, had been shot down. "His luck finally ran out," she said. "It's terrible for the Bong family."

An odd thing happened, too. Arthur's picture–the one he had taken showing him broadly grinning and wearing his army fatigues and helmet, inexplicably fell off the top of the piano.

It was well into June before the telegram arrived. Whoever received it at the telegraph office must have known Dad would be at work in the Memorial Building and had it delivered there instead of home.

When Dad took the envelope, he happily announced to everyone in the office that it must be from Arthur, and everyone joked he must need money.

But no. The telegram began, "We regret to inform you..."

I don't know how Dad reacted. I never heard exactly.

But he must have cried out, perhaps dropping the hideous telegram to the floor. The smiling faces of the office staff must have turned to looks of horror, and they must have gathered around him, their arms supporting him, saying, "Art! Art! What is it?"

The news must have spread through the Memorial Building like wildfire. Dad was a self-controlled person. But he must have collapsed in agony. Perhaps he called out Arthur's name. Perhaps he kept saying, "I can't believe it. I can't believe it. He was coming home."

Yet, in spite of everything, he must have thought, "Oh, God. How to tell Mama."

He managed to get to his car, telling everyone he could make it. He drove to Mansfield Street to get Aunt Bertha to come to the house with him.

And the two of them drove the few blocks to Sutherland Street.

I was upstairs sitting in the big rocker by the front window reading "All This and Heaven Too " thinking I would use it for a book report when I got to ninth grade in the fall, even though Miss Goudie, the almost legendary high school English teacher I hoped I would get, usually wouldn't allow you to give a book report on a book that had been made into a movie.

Mother was washing clothes in the basement.

Mary Elizabeth was outside hanging clothes on the clothes reel.

It was a gorgeous June day, perfectly fitting one of Dad's favorite bits of poetry, "Oh, what is so rare as a day in June, if ever come perfect days?"

I saw the car pull up in front and Dad get out. Strange that he would be home in the middle of the morning. Then Aunt Bertha got out. Stranger yet that she would be with him. There was something odd about their manner. They weren't speaking, and Aunt Bertha was holding a handkerchief to her mouth.

They came in the front door. There were voices. I heard the basement door open. More voices, and I thought I heard Dad say Junior's name.

Then screams and screams and more screams.

After all these years, only impressions of those first few hours remain in my mind.

Whenever anything happened, my first instinct was to tell Aunt Carrie. So I ran down the street and burst in the front door. Aunt Carrie, her hair in curlers as usual, was listening to her soap opera on the radio. Geraldine was combing her hair at the kitchen sink. "Junior's been killed!" I shouted, and then ran back up the street. Clara May, next door, must have seen me, and came out to see what was happening.

Aunt Carrie came running, and then Geraldine. I had never seen Geraldine cry before. Soon other neighbors were standing outside on the sidewalk. People from Dad's office came. Mrs. Pollari from up the street--she was a nurse--came in the back door to see if she could help. Someone called

Aunt Mary in Ashland, and Aunt Mabel came--and Mrs. Bowles, and Mrs. Oliver, the mother of Arthur's friend, Buddy.

Mother lay prostrate on the couch, clutching Arthur's army portrait, moaning and weeping and calling out his name. Someone called Dr. O'Brian, who soon came and gave her some medicine. I must have been standing, shivering, near the door in the hall when the doctor left. He glanced over at me and said to Dad, "It's hard on the children, too." Dad, standing near the front door, sobbing into his handkerchief, nodded his head.

Then he gathered Mary Elizabeth and me in his arms and said, "Now all we have is you."

But Mother didn't notice us. She only kept calling for Arthur. More people began to come in. Mr. Bennett, our minister, came and attempted to console Mother, but she wouldn't listen. "No, No," she cried out to him.

Rejected, he stood in the front hallway and prayed.

Later Uncle George came in from the Geneva Mine, where he worked, and Uncle Joe, who also worked at the Geneva. Later still, Uncle Harry and Aunt Eva came from Wakefield, and Mother said to Aunt Eva through her sobbing that she always thought it was so horrible when their little Jane died so many years ago.

No details of Arthur's death were known then, of course; but in the frenzy of grief, Mother thought of the old German man Arthur had befriended, and she thought about how the picture had fallen off the piano. She thought about the Bong family, too.

More people came to the house, but most were not allowed to see Mother, who had been taken upstairs to her bedroom. But the indomitable Mrs. Thacker, the corsetiere--not all that close a friend--barged upstairs anyway and tried to console Mother, telling her she must be strong for Mary Elizabeth and me and she must accept the mysterious ways of God.

Mother was not so far gone in her grief that she couldn't resent the intrusions and the unwanted remarks. Strangely, later that evening, as she sat on the edge of her bed, while Aunt Mary, who had been driven down from Ashland by somebody, tried to comfort her, Mother found enough spunk to heap invectives on the intrusive Mrs. Thacker. "All she knows how to do, anyway, is to push fat up and push fat down and then push it up again. We all laughed--even Mother herself.

Several days later, Joel Stein, Arthur's close friend, came to the house. He was the only friend of Arthur's Mother would see. He sat by the side of her bed and held her hand, but said nothing. He only wept.

For weeks and weeks, the nights were the worst. I would lie awake listening for Mother's moans to begin, which they did almost every night. Dad and Aunt Mary would walk her up and down the hallway.

Aunt Mary stayed for nearly a month, and Dad managed to go back to work. Mother gradually got back on her feet and began to move about the house. But for many months she never went outside, except to take a ride in the car. Her hair began to fall out. She attended none of the school events Mary Elizabeth and I were in, not even "The Mikado" my senior year, when I played Pooh Bah.

Any young person's death is a tragedy. No parent loses a child easily, no matter its age. But to Mother and Dad,

Arthur's death was, I think, particularly difficult to accept because of the kind of person he was. As his letters reflect, he was so bursting with life, so full of enthusiasm, optimism, and good will, so intelligent, so graced with what Mother always called "a wonderful philosophy of life," so brimming with plans for the future--it didn't seem possible that he now lay cold and dead in a faraway grave, all that exuberant, youthful promise now gone.

But it was, and our lives would never be the same.

In fact, it would be three or four years before Mother would begin to go out at all. But one Sunday, to the amazement of all, she managed to go to church and make it through the service, and very gradually she began to take up her church and community activities. Eventually, she even went through the chairs at Eastern Star again, and once again became president of the stately Ironwood Women's Club. Her community activities even won her a place in "Who's Who in American Women."

But for the rest of her life, she never spoke Arthur's name, and none of us ever said his name again in her presence--and seldom to each other. Even now, more than fifty years later, it is difficult for me to say the name "Arthur."

Voices of Michigan

A Great Tradition

Andrew K. Watkins

The mist slowly rises off the dew-laden field. The freshly painted white lines glisten. The maize and blue block M dominates mid-field. The feeling in the air is an indescribable mixture of pride, tradition, anticipation, tension, and, of course, football. The setting is an autumn Saturday in southeastern Michigan and, more importantly, in Ann Arbor. The University of Michigan Wolverines have a home football game today, and everyone knows it. They can feel it. The people of the area know the great tradition and all its rituals.

Andrew K. Watkins was born and raised in Grosse Pointe, MI. He is a senior at University Liggett School where he enjoys playing sports and participating in student government. He also enjoys traveling, golfing and scuba diving. **Andrew** will enter Princeton University this fall.

With my stomach in knots mostly from nerves, I wake earlier on football Saturdays than on other Saturdays. I feel this way even though I am not on the team. This is the sign of a true fan, one that lives and dies on how the team performs. There is a feeling of exuberant joy when the team wins and unbelievable sorrow when they lose. On football Saturdays, I carefully go through a specific routine making sure to follow all my personal superstitions. I wear the same shirt every weekend until the shirt's luck runs out, and I always take the same items to the game: a Michigan

213

football and the media guide. I know in the back of my mind I have no real influence on the game, but I do it anyway. I have to.

We leave early enough to have plenty of time to tailgate even if the freeway is crowded. As we drive, I see the flags flying above the doorways on the houses, and on this day they don't represent pride for a state or country; today it is pride for a football team. Many of the cars on the freeway are also adorned with Michigan flags flapping as they race to the stadium. I know that today all roads lead to Ann Arbor. We stop at The Bagel Factory to buy our lunch. These are not average bagels; these bagels show the true colors of Wolverine spirit. On football Saturdays, the bagels are maize and blue.

Upon arriving at the golf course to park, we set up our maize table with blue chairs and a tablecloth with a football field printed on it. Anywhere else this setup would seem excessive, but here it is perfect. We eat our lunch while glancing through the media guide to answer today's WJR trivia question and to check the statistics of prior games with today's rival. In between the rows of cars on the golf course, there are games of pickup football, lawn bowling, and some putting on the greens. I often join in a game of football. It doesn't matter if I know the other participants in the game, as long as you bleed maize and blue, you are welcome.

We leave the golf course about forty-five minutes before game time, plenty of time to participate in all the pre-game activities. Nearly every person there is outfitted in maize and blue. An occasional fan from the opposing team is seen but quickly swallowed back into the sea of maize and blue. We file through the gates with 111,000 of our closest friends. The great tradition and history is palpable. I enter through the threshold into the stadium. We call it the Big House. Just hearing the name, the pride is visible on the faces of Wolverine fans, and the fear is apparent in opponents. Even after all these years, I am overwhelmed by the sheer size. People entering for the first time often have to stop and catch their breath because they are awestruck and mutter something about its enormity. If you have never been there, it is impossible to understand.

I find my seat: Section 10, Row 48, Seat 10. The same seat for the past sixteen years. I have attended most games since I was born, and if I live in the area when I am an adult, probably will attend most games until I die. We greet the people sitting around us; they have sat there as long as I can remember. The people behind us complain because their son is getting married next Saturday. They are not mad that he is getting married, but that he chose to do it on a day when Michigan has a home game. The man that sits in front of my dad is in his mid-eighties and can barely walk. He never misses a game. These people have the spirit of a true Michigan fan.

The announcer's voice booms over the PA, and the 235-member marching band takes the field. I know they will play the greatest fight song ever written. All the maize and blue faithful rise and join in a rousing course of "The Victors." "Hail to the victors valiant. Hail to the conqu'ring heroes." The words ring true for the team, but there is also a feeling that builds inside me when I hear these words, and it makes me feel like a hero. The M Club brings its banner out and hoists it over mid-field. I can see the maize and blue winged helmets in the tunnel. The captains' fists thrust into the air, and they charge out of the tunnel under the banner; each player leaping toward the sky to touch the banner. I have often dreamed what it must be like to make that leap. It is game time. All the talk about the game in the media during the preceding week has built to this point, the opening kickoff, and the game begins.

Michigan makes a great play. I prepare my hand knowing the man in front of me will turn around to slap me a high five. He always does. 111,000 fists fly into the air as we sing while the band plays "The Victors." At half-time the band does another performance. Often they play "Temptation" and, as every Wolverine fan knows, you can't have one without the other, so the band follows with, "The Hawaiian War Chant." The second half begins, and by now the Wolverines are usually ahead. It is a glorious atmosphere. On the rare occasion when the team loses, it is obvious by the sorrow on the dejected faces exiting the stadium. In my heart, I am sure the team will recover next week. Win or lose, there is still a feeling of pride that I have been cheering for a great team.

Football Saturdays in Ann Arbor are a tradition like no other I know. Many people from southeastern Michigan attend games most fall Saturdays year after year; it is still exciting even after so long. People from other places sometimes cannot understand this ritual. I tell them that it gives me a great feeling inside and a sense of pride that I get from nothing else. To me and to many others, these traditions are more than just football. They are a way of life. There is nothing I would rather do on an autumn weekend than go to a Michigan football game.

POETRY

LITTLE SABLE POINT

Voices of Michigan

Glen David Young, a long time resident of northern Michigan, splits his time between Petoskey and Mackinac Island. After many years as a teacher in Alanson, Michigan, Glen has recently transferred to and is currently teaching English at Petoskey High School. Young is the recipient of a National Endowment For The Humanities Fellowship and is writing a new Literate Matters column for the Petoskey News Review.

Waterstone

There is little in the way he shuffles through the
cramped room,
unless it is the worn side of his flannel slippers.
There is nothing in the way he speaks in tongues,
unless it is the transparent features of his motionless
face.
What there was is now stone, breaking time that flows
around the sides of his water world, now at ebb tide.

When he lies face down his own photograph on the
cherry wood end table, the wheels of our conjecture
spin
counterclockwise past the wheels of our concern;
the family he has separated from parts also like the
water.
His speech tells tales of long ago, lost on us now.

He spits out disjointed images of fertile soil,
heaped beside the Locks, amid ore carriers and
mail bags. A wide broken grin stares back across fifty

years of broken marriages, grandchildren, funerals
and pill bottles.

Thin Irish lips spoke clarity then; dark Roman eyes
looked down midnights into the garden, howling
out expletives rubbed from drunken ruins.
A lawn chair in the middle of the broken driveway,
where the children sang songs of Grandma Grunt.

Steady hands, long fingers, sorted mail, pounded
nails, pulled weeds, raised whiskey glasses.
Thin legs walked mailman miles, ran hedgerows
after deer, jumped troubled ditches. Wild hair
warmed wilder ideas, hatched ever blooming
schemes aimed at better, better, better.
Waterstone now.

Stuttering ideas weigh paper light, brought down
about trembling fingers, callused, bruised, weak.
He folds out of sight his own photograph, not reminded of
what was, so much as what is not.
He declines his medication these days, headstrong
in his rheumy decline, slipping from the undulating
reef.

His collapsing form rocks back and forth, side to side,
standing headlong into the current, washed over
again and again, like the rock that breaks the flow, until it
is broken itself, a part of the flow.

- Glen David Young

Nancy Deckinga grew up in Ohio, later lived 14 years in Latin America and freelanced for **Business Mexico**, a publication of the American Chamber of Commerce in Mexico City. Ten years ago, Michigan became home. **The Tool Box** is the first poem to slip beyond the confines of her personal journal.

The Tool Box

The tool box, shiny, rarely used
sat on the workbench.
The tools inside, like new, were off-limits for the
boy.

The canvas bag, filled with newspapers
lay on the garage floor.
Beside it, the boy fretted over his bike's flat tire.
His old pliers stripped the nuts as he took them off.

The boy took a new wrench
to make the job faster.
The father walked in and didn't understand
so he yelled.
The boy put the wrench back in the tool box,
but locked the hurt in his heart.

Now, the father is old.
Now, the boy is a man
with money
and tools
and the hurt in his heart.

The old man is dying
and now understands
the value of the son is more than
the tool
and a broken spirit more costly
than a broken wrench
and harder to replace.

"The tool box goes to Ryan," he says.
And he means it as reconciliation.

But the son doesn't understand
that the value of the father is more than
the guarded hurt.

"I don't want that old thing," he says.

- Nancy Deckinga

Kim Beach is the co-captain of the *Chit Chat*, a fictitious sailboat
that was created in 1994 by Kim and her co-captain and best friend
Cathy who she met while working on the Island at Little Bobs in
1983. The *Chit Chat* has *sailed* each year bringing various friends
to enjoy the camaraderie of Mackinac Island.

The Maiden's Voyage

Each year we set sail on a "maiden" voyage of sort,
To the island of Mackinac, the most magical port.
Our boat was fondly christened as we sat on the docks;
The CHIT CHAT was launched over vodka, tonic and rocks.
It's an all-female crew that completes the ship's log;
Our seamanship equal to the saltiest dog.
Sailors at sea, we chart the course of our lives;
The manifest a blend of friends, mothers and wives.
With a mission of fun, the "living seas" we do roam,
But each year in July, the CHIT CHAT sails home.
On the deck of the boat we share laughter and tears;
We tell stories of life and reveal our deep fears.
The voyage is deemed therapy by all the crew members.
Our spirits renewed by the spark of friends' embers.
The CHIT CHAT is more than a boat that's not here,
It's a celebration of life and those people we hold dear.
The bridge is in sight now, we'll race to the shores;
The CHIT CHAT sails in as the bold cannon roars.
As she glides through the docks and comes to rest in her slip,
We are thankful for our journey aboard this "friend" ship.

- Kim Beach

223

Voices of Michigan

Now 50, **Frederic Sibley** has been writing poetry since he turned 15. His work has been published in England and Japan as well as the United States, and it has won him several awards. He taught composition at the community-college level for many years.

37/75

You were my age (half your years now)
When I arrived,
And I can still look in your eyes.
But we are not mountains, which think nothing of time,
Though the earth beneath them erupt.

When we took that unmarked trail today,
The summit cheated us.
For the path just vanished in underbrush,
And the peak was lost
To a stand of fir.

Yet I was proud of us.
Bum knees and all,
We would have bushwhacked through
Had our shadows not fallen
So long on the late spring snow.

Father,
What western ridge awaits our step
Even as this old sun sets?

June 1987
Mount Baker

Catching the Falling

for Chris

Early on, the evening showed its teeth

In dragon tongues of lightning.

But after those soundless flashes,

Whatever the heavens were threatening

They held their fire,

Leaving the ceiling so clear

That when the star-shower started,

Meteors burst like snowballs

Out of the blackness and back--

For all the split-seconds we could see.

- Frederic Sibley

Bonnie Flaig and her husband, Mike, daughter and son, Katie and Wil, plus two cats, Festus and Tonto, have returned to Minnesota to be near extended family and to enjoy record snow falls!! Bonnie, who last year was on faculty at Kalamazoo Valley Community College, is now teaching at Rochester Community and Technical College in Rochester, Minnesota.

New Ulm, Minnesota

Your song is a lonely wail of a freight train,
the clack-clack of wheels pulling into
a station where nothing is new.
I carry you with me,
your music, an old photograph of
a threshing crew, stout women
hefting steaming bowls to a picnic table,
and always, somewhere in the photo, maybe
next to the wagon piled high,
a little brass band playing music. *Music.*
Uncles, maybe neighbors, who hauled
concertinas and trumpets across the Atlantic,
up the Minnesota River,
as if the music could lessen the sting of
the work, summer's oppressive heat, the
impossible winters.

You are my German grandfather learning
to waltz behind his plow, the horse
pulling the blade through stubborn soil,
Grandpa behind steering and 1-2-3, 1-2-3
with his feet to make the job easier.
His rows wandered like breathless children,
twirl here, misstep there, but think
of a man dancing with his plow, a man

227

who would die young, 58, during the
kind of blizzard that made settlers regret
choosing this open prairie. When he failed
to return to the house, Grandma followed the guide rope
they'd hung from house to barn,
freezing fingers, hand-over-hand,
and found him face down in the cowstall *(Kuhstahl, dear.*
Say it in German.)

New Ulm, I love you and hate you, too. You are
worn, but sturdy houses; meticulous, working class
lawns; pale lederhosen; and a green cap with a single
feather. You are streudel and sauerbraten, bratwurst,
beer. You are a galloping polka that makes my
lungs hurt. You are "The Jolly Lumberjacks" and
"The Six Fat Dutchmen." You are
a place in history where white settlers
moved in next to and on top of Sioux Indians who tried to
live in peace with you, later called you a word that meant
"bad neighbors" and made fun of your hairy faces.
You killed them without remorse. They were starving that
winter and so might you, if you didn't defend
what was yours.

Oh, and who am I to call you on it now? Who am I but
a German-Irish daughter who grew up with your
privileges, loved music, lived by it, profited
from it. Worked hard, played hard. *Ach ya. Ach du.*
New Ulm as tinny concertina music and cold Schell's beer.
New Ulm on guard against marauders, against
those foreigners (Norwegians) over in Hanska.

Echoey George's Ballroom, Schnitzelbank,
Kaiserhoff. Wherever I go, you are

there making me vigilant, making me keep
the beat, making me crave beer in my second
pregnancy, making me dream of red geraniums in
brown window boxes. You call me home to walk
these broken sidewalks. *How ya doin', hey?*
To listen to stories of grandfathers who kill
themselves over bad land prices--*Ach du lieber!*--sons who
burn their houses for insurance money.

All this, and I still think I have something to say.
New Ulm, you are home
to my poet friend Eddie saying "Forget
trying to say something. Go for the music. *The music.*"

New Ulm as balm.
New Ulm as psalm.
New Ulm as St. Mary's Catholic church,
incense and landjaggers cooking with potato salad
in the basement.
You buried my father, New Ulm, and married my mother.
Oh, Oedipus. Oh, German settlement.
Oh, Hermanstraum pageant each July. Oh, Goosetown gang
fighting the Wallerchei gang, south side versus the north side.

From six hundred miles away, you still play
me like a concertina, someone's knee bouncing,
someone's thump-thump-thump on a wooden floor.
And me, singing those strange, hopping rhythms,
singing those awkward, heart-breaking melodies
until my last note fades in the cool air
just outside of town, past the tracks, somewhere
over that ancient Minnesota River.

-Bonnie Flaig

Voices of Michigan

Twice married and twice widowed, **Beatrice Heller Brewer** was born in
Flint in 1916 and now lives in Birch Run, Michigan. Her son and his
wife live in Beulah, Michigan, and her daughter and her family live in
New Hampshire. Beatrice is retired from the Michigan Civil Service,
and she is enjoying writing poetry and is a life member of the National
Society of Poets.

The Cobbler

In the palm of my hand is a scratched and faded tin-type-
  a mystery
surviving through the years to inspire the story of its
  history.
Studio posed, before a muted scene,
sits a man with serious mien.
His shirt in patterned calico
has no collar, sleeves rolled at elbow.
A leather apron hangs in folds,
with knees and hand a shoe he holds,
while a knife is in his right hand grip,
poised to trim a leather strip
from the shoe to show his labors,
so his heirs will know
he was a cobbler, mender of shoes,
and would be proud if son would choose
to follow in his father's trade.
My grandfather's tin-type thus portrayed,
the saga of his early life in 'tin',
before the family moved from Canada to Michigan.

                              - Beatrice Heller Brewer

Voices of Michigan

As a mother and a special education teacher, **Jodi L. Burkett** knows the importance of the self-discovery and self-confidence of a child. However, having been overstimulated by gadgets, toys and technology, a child rarely explores his own internal resources. Jodi encourages children to look inside themselves...no batteries required!

One Place

Grampi saw me droopy.
"Can't you find it, Princess?"
"Find what, Grampi?"
He peeked behind my ear. "Not here."
"Then where?"
He wondered. I wondered too.
"I'll help you find it. It can't be far."
I lifted my feet and looked under my seat.
"Grampi, what does it look like?"
"Oh, it's small but very big, too." His knees bent low, then he
        began to grow.
"Grampi, you look high and I'll look low."
So, he looked. I looked, too.
Grampi searched the tree. I crawled on my knees.
"Not here."
"Then where?"
I patted the sand sugar off my knee and heard a humming bee.

"Grampi, what noise does it make?"
"Sometimes it's sneaky-quiet and sometimes it's recess-loud." His
        hands clapped and jumped back.
Then, he listened. I listened, too.
Making elephant ears, we waited. I followed a bee. He sat
        quietly.

"Not here."

"Then where?"

I rubbed Dandelion butter on my nose and bent to tickle my toes.

"Grampi, what does it feel like?"

It's like a warm, fresh towel right out of the drier." His summer-
        pink arms wrapped me.

He snuggled. I snuggled, too.

"Are you hiding it, Grampi?"

I peeked up his sleeve, not sure I should believe.

"Not here."

"Then where?"

I breathed in the windblown smell of Grampi's cologne.

"Grampi, what does it smell like?"

"It smells like mom's perfume and Christmas time."

He winked. I just blinked and closed my eyes to think with my
        nose.

"Grampi, we've looked and we've listened and we've sniffed. If
        it's not here, then where?"

"There's only one place left to look, because it's always been right
        here."

"We should have looked here first, Grampi?"

"Always look here first, Princess." He held my hand on my heart.

"This is the only place to search. You hold all the happiness
        you'll ever need!"

"My happy is inside me, Grampi?"

"Yes, Princess. Always."

He smiled. I smiled, too.

- Jodi L. Burkett

234

Sharon Frost is a core member of Visions of Peace Drum and Dance Company and has practiced the healing art of Occupational Therapy for14 years. She is a member of the Women's Journey Group and founder of the Women's Book Group of Petoskey. Sharon is married with two little ones...an honor and a roller coaster ride of a lifetime!

Dance and Drum Circle

The transfer of heat -
        from hand to drum -
        from foot to floor
The sound and movement begin.

A beat, a stomp, a tap, a flutter -
        together or apart -
A stirring, a rise ...
        A promise to the soul.

Ancient, modern, primal -
        tapping into longings, remembrance -
        or boring right to the core.

Emotion makes way through sound,
vibration, visual clarity or blurs -
        fine tuned, widely ranged ...
        Or nothing at all.

Attachment to instruments -
with history through time -
        meanings both subtle and fierce.

Or a casual loan that is accepted with respect -
     always.

The body yields, resists, flows, charges,
extends, startles, hides -
     penetrates, withdraws ...
never offering an apology to the moment.

A convergence of trust, inspiration,
     abandonment -
     or deliberate consideration.

Indeed, the transfer of heat -
     from hand to drum -
     from foot to floor.

- Sharon Frost

~~~

Dedicated to the individuals in the Visions of Peace Drum and
Dance Company of Petoskey, Michigan. A breeze of strength,
dignity and creativity, caressing the waters of Lake Michigan and
our community.

Beryl Bonney-Conklin is a poet, an author of children's stories and a professional artist. She has had several of her works of poetry published in various magazines in Michigan. Since **Beryl** retired from teaching, she has been drawn in the direction of writing poetry and children's stories.

Things I Meant to Tell You After We Were Old

About the fit of you against my skin
so familiar but still a mystery to my hand.
I thought to tell you
the importance of first light
as I often saw it fall
across the tumbled sheets of night.
Instead I would slip away
caught doing daily mundane things
leaving words for some other time.

Before I could ever catch the breath of you
or establish a where or why,
the fading began.
Like old photographs exposed too long
our edges blurred
and we never did grow old
together.

I can only dream your skin remembers
as mine
after some pale dawn.

- Beryl Bonney-Conklin

Voices of Michigan

Molly McDonald is 20 years old and has lived in Kalamazoo for most of her life. She is a student at Oberlin College in Oberlin, Ohio where she is pursuing an English major with a concentration in creative writing.

Pie

She once made a pie with only
three small, hard green apples.
So it wasn't much of a pie,

really, mostly thick, flaky crust.
Perhaps that was all she had,
or maybe she was simply

rationing the fruit,
a carryover from the days
when fresh fruit was a rare luxury.

Or maybe she lost her mind
momentarily, a first indication
of the dementia that was to follow
so many years later.

The daughters-in-law love
to retell this story, laughing,
sometimes changing it from apples

to pears, because the details aren't
important, really, just as long
as they prove her fallibility,

she, who always kept plastic
slipcovers on the davenports, and
served supper promptly at six.

- Molly McDonald

S. K. Ellis was born in the late seventies to a working-class suburban family. From the age of nine, she began to write stories and poems in spare moments. Ellis teaches residents of Detroit how to read, plus she is involved in a writer's support group at Barnes and Noble Booksellers.

Portrait of the Artist's Heart Breaking

I thought of you today.
It's been too long since we've last been engaged in
conversation,
and what a wonderful conversation.
You, adorning a composed stare,
and me with my tablet and pencil.
Really, there was little spoken between us,
as I sketched you and you begged to see the
resemblance.
And the resonance later, in the bedroom,
the stare still on your face,
as I undressed with little reservation.
When you sighed in my ear and told me
that you could no longer wait, and we didn't,
and you told me you loved me,
I became a dupe under your touch.
I also remembered how I leaned against the railing at the
train station,
And I waited for you,
but you never arrived.
And that's what I thought of today,

when my mind traced the images of your face
I remembered everything; the length of your jaw line, the
defiant blue of your eyes, the arch of your brows, the
chiseled straightness to your nose, everything down to the
dimples in your cheeks.
You were alive in my mind today when I thought back,
your smile haunting me to the tune of agony.
And every attempt I could make at the time to capture you
in a haste of violent oils of brown and green and blue and
gold, pencil or paint, charcoal or crayon,
Never quite came close to the spirit of you, and the
surprise you were to me each and every day.
Making love to you in my mind, in our bedroom,
During that rainstorm,
So, so long ago,
Makes me now wonder, where can you be?
What company are you keeping-or are you alone?
Do you ever call out my name, or reach for me during the
night,
perhaps during a random rain shower?
Do you ever think of me?
Do you love me still?
Do you still have the portrait?
Am I going mad?
Will you ever come home?

- S. K. Ellis

Jennifer Marlow "officially" began writing poetry while in college although she thinks she has always thought and written in poems. Currently Jennifer is working on her Master's degree in the creative writing program at Northern Michigan University. She is paying for her education by teaching English composition to the first year college students, and loving it!

from far away

we were at york
beach, and i
was drifting far away
from you. i was little
then, but you became smaller
as your frantically waving hand
was barely visible
from my rubber raft.
i wasn't afraid
of the wide ocean
pulling me, pulling me.
it was only when i looked back,
back at the slowly receding shoreline,
back where you became mirage
all water and sand
then i was frightened
with the unanswered question.
why did i make it out as far as i did,
without my even knowing?
somehow i made my return to you

that day. though the ocean seemed stronger
than my busily paddling arms
with rubber burns and scrapes on the skin
rarely exposed to the light.

tomorrow you will board
at logan airport, and i
will wait down here for you
among the ant hill mountains
and centipede tractor trailer trucks.
i'll be barely visible
from up there.
but we both know
i'm bigger than life now
or at least i try to be.
i prepare for your visit,
the grown-up daughter
always prepared to paddle her way
in any direction, every direction.
but you will see lake superior
before you see me
and maybe you'll remember
the day i floated
without direction, out of your reach.
and maybe you'll think
how airplanes and little rubber rafts
take us places.

- Jennifer Marlow

Debbie Olson Frontiera grew up in Lake Linden, Michigan, teaches kindergarten in Houston, Texas and spends her summers in a cottage on Rice Lake, Michigan. She has self-published a collection of poetry and short words entitled ***Through My Eyes***.

Mosquito

Familiar whine in my ear
You settle on my forearm
Prepare to pierce my skin with your proboscis
I raise my hand to strike.

Wait!
What if I let you complete the cycle?
You might feed the songbird
Who cheers my day.

Your larvae might feed the minnow
Who feeds the fingerling
Who feeds the pike
Who feeds me.

You might be a meal for the brown bat
Whose guano fertilizes
Tomatoes for my salad.

SMACK!

But not today.

                - Debbie Olson Frontiera

Voices of Michigan

"Doc" is a retired chiropractor who summers on Mackinac Island and winters in San Antonio, Texas. A regular contributor to San Antonio's *Sun Poetic Times*, Doc is additionally the author of three chatbooks: ***Magic Thing, Changing Shirts on the Road,*** and *-Shipshape.* He has also published the ***Doc Song Book.***

Rookies

Sit.
Stay.
Heel.

The most often used commands
With young dogs. Or boys.

Tails and tongues wagging,
Left and right,
Ahead and back,
Behind, lagging.

Tasting, claiming,
Discovering everything!

Larking, barking:
"It's mine! It's mine! It's mine!"

Life's shellfish adventure
Strung with pleasure's pearls:

"A treasure!"

"A playmate!"
"A friend!"

Our "Woof"
Of reproof

Brings them
Tail-tucked
Repentant to

Nuzzle our knees,
Hide their heads
Between our legs.

They cannot hear
The love and fear

In the Patriarch Bark

That knows too well
Of skunks and poison ivy,

Of porcupines,

Of BEARS.

- "Doc"

Linda Burton Parish was born in Austria and fell in love with Upper Michigan when she first camped there in 1957. Her Ojibwa husband and she have six children and nine grandchildren. Linda has been published in the **Woods-Runner** and **Toronto Native Times**.

Ojibwa Woman

Ojibwa woman walk in my dream
Under the great shade canopy of leaves
Where the speckled sun does not
dance on the ground,
I wait to speak to you of bravery
as you leave.

Your fear beats like a drum
in my breast
And the words of bravery fall
like dust from my mouth.

Bi-gebezhin ndoo-nikaang ndoo-binoojiinsim[1]
Softly your grandmothers sway and
sing your welcome through my mouth.
Your departing sweet smile
I never forget.

Miigwetch[2] blows the wind.

- Linda Burton Parish

Translations courtesy of instructors and students of the Ojibwa Language Institute at Bay Mills Community College

---

[1]English translation: lie in my arms my baby
[2]English translation: thank you

Voices of Michigan

Laurie A. Cerny's photography, feature articles and poetry have appeared in numerous horse publications. Her work, including *Galloping Ghosts - Ghostly Horse Stories for Young Readers*, has received top honors by both Michigan Press Women and the National Federation of Press Women. She also has published a book of horse poetry entitled *Literally Horses.*

Trail Ride

Shod hooves
crush little
yellow elm leaves
along the road
like spoon to
corn flakes against
my earthenware
cereal bowl.

Into the woods
brown oak leaves
rustle like water
falling over moss
covered rocks;
the rushing noise
causing her
to shy.

251

After an hour
stirrups dropped
we rest under
an apple tree
biting into the
Red Delicious flesh
that grew like
love all summer.

- Laurie A. Cerny

Laura K. Drahozal, a lifelong Michigander, met her husband, Steve, on Mackinac Island. They currently live in Farmington where Laura is an activities director and art teacher. As a Farmington Jaycee, Laura won the Michigan Jaycee Write UP essay competition in 1995 and the national competition in 1996.

Two A.M.

I stir awake, cold at two a.m.
I have kicked the blankets off again.
I grope at my knees
and yank the comforter to my chin.
Like a newborn puppy with blind instinct,
I crawl into the warmth of your body.
I slowly stretch my leg along yours,
Feeling your warm skin with my smooth, cool leg.
My toes caress your sole.
My fleshy hip laps against your hard thigh.
Your sweaty shoulder dampens my cheek
as I smell your musky scent.
Your deep, even breathing
sounds like ocean waves breaking over rocks.
The rhythm lulls me back to sleep.

- Laura K. Drahozel

Voices of Michigan

APPENDICES

TEMPORARY VACANCY
LAKE MICHIGAN SHORELINE

The Publishers

Mary Jane Barnwell and **Jane Harrell Winston** met on Mackinac Island, Michigan and discovered they both shared a dream. Mary Jane was interested in publishing a book; Jane was interested in conducting a writing contest. And thus began *Voices of Michigan...an Anthology of Michigan's Finest New Authors.* A publishing company was needed, so they decided to form their own. They combined Mackinac and their names and became MackinacJane's Publishing Company. The rest is what is known as "history." It is hoped that you, the authors, and you the readers enjoy the two volumes and the writings within as much as Mary Jane and Jane have enjoyed running the contest and publishing the book.

Mary Jane, a Michigander born in Detroit, spent summers on Mackinac Island. She has degrees in Nutrition from Northern Michigan and Wayne State Universities and currently she and husband, Roman, and their three-year-old son, Willie, live in Petoskey. Mary Jane co-owns and helps manage the Island Bookstores of Mackinac Island and Mackinaw City. A lover of book selling, she always wanted to be involved in the publishing of a book. Realizing she would never be a published author, she decided she could help others fulfill their dreams to become published authors.

Jane, born and reared in Bloomington, IN married an Air Force officer after graduating from Indiana University and traveled with John and Uncle Sam for the next 30 years. They currently live in Warner Robins, Georgia in the winter and on Mackinac Island, Michigan in the summer. Jane is a faculty member of Fort Valley State University in Fort Valley, GA where she teaches in the College of Education. A grown daughter, Jamie Sue Stanzione, a grown son, John Jeffrey Winston, six grandchildren and two cats round out the Winston household.

The Artists

Mary Hramiec-Hoffman, as a child growing up in Petoskey and Harbor Springs, Michigan resort areas surrounded by Lake Michigan's Little Traverse Bay, was always drawing. Encouraged by her artistically-inclined parents, her drawing ability took on a life of its own. She was enrolled in children's art classes at North Central Michigan College and the Mc Cune Arts Center in Petoskey by the time she was nine years old.

Mary continued to develop her talent and obtained her degrees in fine art from St. Thomas Aquinas College and Kendall College of Art and Design. After graduating Mary held the position of creative director at an advertising agency.

Beyond the beauty of the Petoskey and Harbor Springs area, Mary draws upon her experiences and memories of traveling the United States with her parents, seven brothers, one sister and the family dog in one of America's first motor homes her father expertly fashioned out of a GM delivery truck.

Known for the delicate sensitivity portrayed in her oil scenes of northern Michigan, Mary's paintings reflect an appreciation of the Fauvist and Impressionist movement; she creates a pulsating vibrance on the surface of her canvases. Behind the spontaneous brushwork and loosely applied colors in her paintings there is control that brings the elements into a structured whole. Collectors appreciate Mary's custom of donating a portion of each sale toward cancer research and charity programs.

Mary still lives in the same scenic resort area where she grew up with her husband and business partner Mark Hoffman. She can be reached at her website www.markenmerry.com or by calling 231.526.1011, her Harbor Springs home office.

257

Some of the sketches featured in *Voices of Michigan* are from a Mackinac Island sketchbook by **Rob Harrell** a freelance illustrator located in Indianapolis, Indiana. To see more of Rob's work, visit his website, www.RobHarrell.com.

Other sketches are by **Karen R. James** who has been drawing since the age of five when she received her first sketch book and colored pencils as a gift. With no formal art training, she accredits her freelance style of drawing a God-given talent. After graduating from the University of Michigan in an unrelated field, she landed a position at a publishing company in Battle Creek as a graphic artist. She went from there to a family-owned print shop where she worked until becoming a mother. Karen is now a stay-at-home mom and daycare provider. She lives in Union City, Michigan with her husband Bryan and her two children Emily and Sam who are her very own aspiring young artists.

Robert Roebuck, the graphic artist for volume two hails from Talladega, Alabama, a small town know for its Civil War battles, stock car racing and the Alabama School for the Deaf. Talladega houses a large deaf community, and Robert's parents are a part of that community. There Robert lived (and drew) along with his younger sister for 19 years.

Professionally Robert has been a graphic designer for 10 years, but he has always been an artist at heart. He won his first coloring contest at age five at the Woolworth's department store in Talladega.

Robert graduated from the Art Institute of Atlanta where he learned to express his ideas on a PC. He currently works for a large national printing company and owns his own design company, Visual Chaos, where he creates brochures, company identities, CD and book covers, magazine ads and flyers. Robert aspires to be one of the great among the great in the advertising world one day.

Robert is married and he and his soul mate, Maria, live in Atlanta, Georgia.

The Editor

Janice Trollinger was born in Waco, Texas, to an Air Force family, so she lived in many cities in Texas, in Roswell, New Mexico (didn't see any aliens or space ships), and even in Nagoya, Japan, before her father retired. She attended Sam Houston Sate University, getting a B.A. majoring in English, minoring in Art. After working for a year, she attended graduate school at the University of Arkansas getting a M.A. in English. Since that time she has taught at several universities across the United State and is currently an Assistant Professor at Fort Valley State University in Fort Valley, Georgia.

Janice credits her talent for and interest in literature to a family of readers who taught her to read before she entered school. A voracious reader of fiction, she believes her editing skills came naturally as a result of a life-long reading habit and a father who, although not formally educated, was a consummate grammarian who always corrected her grammar. Through him, she derived much of her love for words and stories. Add to that her many years of teaching freshman composition where she served as an "editor" to her students, and it is easy to see how she would up as an editor for ***Voices of Michigan.***

The Readers/Judges

David Abbey learned of the need for readers by visiting the *Voices* website and volunteered to read fiction for us. Davis is a lifelong resident of Michigan as he was born in Grand Rapids and has lived in Southwest Michigan since 1961. He is a graduate of Michigan State University, a retired school teacher and an avid skier.

Anne Beaty had a non-fiction piece in volume I of *Voices of Michigan*, was eager to serve as a reader of poetry for volume II. Anne is a native of New York, has lived in California since 1970. An autodidactic, Anne has worked with learning handicapped teenagers for 10 years and now is happily ensconced at an independent bookstore in the Los Angeles area. She spends summers on Mackinac Island and dreams of moving there full time one day.

Jerry Brown read fiction for this contest. Jerry describes herself as a late-blooming Libra transplanted to Georgia following graduate school. She is passionate about learning, writing, reading, horses and friendship. She has Patsy Cline and Handle alternating on the CD-player and watches Buffy, NYPD Blue and Stargate SG-1 without fail. Jerry loves to cook and enjoys good food in the company of like-minded friends. She has recently moved to Omaha, Nebraska from Georgia and is anxiously waiting to see if Nebraska winters are as cold as she fears.

Suzanne Davis is a Marketing Coordinator for the largest Real Estate Company in Kentucky and Southern Indiana. She attended Indiana University, enjoys traveling and has spent many summers on Mackinac Island with her family. Her other hobbies include reading, going to the movies, playing a darn good game of volleyball and horseback riding. Suzi was a fiction reader for the contest and currently lives in Louisville, Kentucky with her husband, two dogs and one cat.

C. T. Duncan, Terry, was a non-fiction reader and has recently publish his own families' history. Terry grew up in Indianapolis, Indiana and has a Bachelors in business and Economics from Indiana University with a minor in literature and a Masters in International Business also from IU. He is retired and has formed Dumar LTD to produce and market technical reports and family histories. Terry is married, has three grown children and three grandchildren.

Julie Chamberlain Foust has been a 5th grade teacher for 22 years and currently is a member of the University Liggett School faculty in Grosse Pointe, Michigan. She is a graduate of Michigan State University. She grew up in East Lansing so spent her summers on the shores of Lake Michigan, sailing port-to-port and always enjoying visits to Mackinac Island. She and her architect husband, Tony, and their almost-grown children love exploring the seasonal beauty at their family retreat in Horton Bay on Lake Charlevoix. Julie has always been active in Junior League, working with children at risk and presenting at national conferences related to child advocacy. Julie was a non-fiction reader for the contest.

Linda Garner currently lives on the Isle of Hope in Savannah, Georgia with her husband, Tim. Linda is a graduate of Tift College, now a part of Mercer University in Macon, GA, in Forsyth, GA. She has both a Bachelor and Master of arts Degree in English and has taught English throughout the United States. Currently Linda is the training director of Gray Line Tours of Savannah, and she enjoys researching and writing new tours. In addition to the *Midnight in the Garden of Good and Evil* tour, she has written tours on Literary Savannah, Movies Made in Savannah and Savannah's Jewish Heritage. Linda and her

Air Force husband were stationed in the Upper Peninsula of Michigan, and she has fond memories of summers of sailing the Michigan Lakes.

Dorothy Hardman is an Assistant Professor in the Department of English and Foreign Languages at Fort Valley State University in Fort Valley, Georgia. Dot earned her Bachelors in English and Art from Wesleyan College, and her Masters in English Education from Mercer University. Both Institutions are located in middle-Georgia. Dot is well-traveled; she presents at many conferences held year-round across the United States, plus she travels outside of the country on behalf of the University nearly every summer. Her most recent travels include a trip to West Africa on a Fulbright Scholarship and to India and Viet Nam as a recipient of a Chancellor's Scholarship. She is currently working on historical fiction based on her study and research in Vietnam. Dorothy read poetry for volume II of **Voices.**

Eileen Hoover lives in Douglas, Michigan where she runs her own business–a shipping and packing counter. She is an accomplished artist and produces works in a variety of mediums including lamp-work glass beads, decorative paper bowls and hand-made clothing accessories. She is a voracious reader and has a book collection approaching a thousand volume covering a multitude of subjects. Her far-flung interests were honed at Eastern Michigan University where she earned a degree in Mathematics and English Literature. She is presently working toward a Masters degree in Computer Science. Eileen was a poetry reader for volume II of **Voices**.

Cathy Kemp lives in Canton, Michigan with her husband, Scott and two sons, Kyle and Colin. She is a graduate of Indiana University with a degree in English. Cathy enjoys cooking, reading and traveling. Cathy was a reader in the non-fiction genre'.

Joan Maril, MSEd, is an Educational Consultant in Austin, Texas. She has developed programs, written curricula and obtained grants in the education field. Included in her work are the videos "Silence is Golden," and "Basic Steps to School Success." In addition to her professional work, Joan has been recognized for her endeavors in both prose and poetry. Joan was one of our non-fiction readers.

Jeaneene Nooney is a transplant from Detroit. She lives and writes in the northern Michigan wood of Kalkaska. A first year author of *Voices of Michigan*, she studied poetry under Dennis Quinn at Northwestern Michigan College. While trying to balance raising her family with writing, she has managed the time to publish newspaper features, poems and is currently working on a novel set in the North. Jeaneene helped us out with volume II as a poetry reader.

Janet Rathke spent summer 1999 in St. Ignace, Michigan where she and her husband, Richard, managed a seasonal motel. When not working at the motel, Janet managed the time to work at the Island Bookstore on Mackinac Island. Janet has a BS in Home Economics Education and a Master of Arts degree in Guidance and Counseling from Eastern Michigan University. She has worked for the Cooperative Extension Service in Michigan, Wisconsin and Minnesota as well as Barnes and Novel Bookstore in Duluth, Minnesota. For as long a she can remember, books and reading have been a part of her life. Janet was a fiction reader.

Wini-Rider Young is a former columnist and Fashion Editor for the *Gazette*, Montreal, Quebec, Canada as well as a former feature writer and women's editor for *The Florida Times-Union*, Jacksonville, Florida. She is currently Editor-at-large and writer for *Water's Edge*, a Florida lifestyle magazine. Wini spent many a summer in her youth at Harbor Springs, Michigan and still retreats there whenever time allows. Wini critiqued our poems for this contest.

Brett Van Emst, originally from Portage, Michigan, grew up in the woos and small streams of norther Michigan. He graduated from Michigan State University and attended the Radcliffe Publishing Course in 1999. 3 a.m. Publishing, a company started by Brett in 1998, released its first book, **I-94:a collection of southwest Michigan writers** (ISBN 0966709705) in October, 1998. He write "The Book Look" for **Directions Magazine** and currently lives on the East Coast where he is employed by Random Publishing House. Brett was a very devoted fiction readers.

Barlekamp, Linda: *Farewell*
Beach, Kim: *The Maiden's Voyage*
Bonney-Conklin, Beryl: *Things I Meant To Tell You After We Were Old*
Brewer, Beatrice Heller: *The Cobbler*
Burkett, Jodi L.: *One Place*
Cerny, Laurie A.: *Trail Ride*
"Doc": *Rookies*
Deckinga, John: *Juan Tesoro*
Deckinga, Nancy: *The Tool Box*
Derrickson, Tom: *Lessons on the AuSable*
Dickman, Shirley L.: *Remembrance*
Dorosh, Debra L.: *The Blue Trees*
Drahozal, Laura K.: *Two A.M,*
Ellis, S. K.: *Portrait of the Artist's Heart Breaking*
Flaig, Bonnie: *New Ulm, Minnesota*
Frontiera, Debbie Olson: *Mosquito*
Frost, Sharon: *Dance and Drum Circle*
Hauge, Chris F.: *Stone Throw Cottage/Betsy's Story*
Heeter, Brian: *Knight Moves: The Internet Connects a Father and His Son*
Hoover, Tom: *Beavers Fly*
LaRocque, Linda: *Uncle Earl's Princess*
Leslie, Roger: *Wise Woman*
Maloney, Sharon Lee: *A Berry Good Lesson*
Marlow, Jennifer: *From Far Away*
McDonald, Molly: *Pie*
Parish, Linda Burton: *Ojibwa Woman*
Propp, Laura S.: *A Fine Day for Varmint Hunting*
Rosewall, Ellen W.: *Ernest Hemingway Sat Here*
Rutherford, R. C.: *The Rare Book*
Sams, Charles: *River Ghost*
Sanwald-Reimanis, Kim: *The Gift*
Scott, Mary Lee: *Midlife Crisis*
Sibley, Frederic: *37/75 and Catching the Falling*
Stuart, Stu: *Paper or Plastic*
Suits, Daniel: *Paul Bunyan's Brother*
Tavernini, Rebecca: *The Zen of Hunting*
Trezise, Robert L.: *Ironwood In War: An Excerpt from "'Up North':A Family Memoir"*
VanBuren, Mike: *To Drown a Memory*
Van Ooyen, Amy J.: *Moving Cloud*
Watkins, Andrew K.: *A Great Tradition*
Young, Glen David: *Waterstone*

Voices of Michigan

Voices of Michigan, order information:

ISBN# 0-9667363-03 - Volume One
ISBN# 0-9667363-11 - Volume Two

*Fax orders: 1 (231) 487-1098
*Telephone orders: 1 (231) 487-1098
*E-mail orders: Macjanes@juno.com
*Postal orders:

> **MackinacJane's Publishing Company**
> *Voices of Michigan*
> 115 State Street
> Petoskey, MI 49770

Pricing:
*Book price $15.95
*Michigan Sales Tax 6% (No tax when shipping out of MI)
*Shipping and handling $4.00. Add $.96 and $1.00
> shipping and handling for each additional book.
> Total for one book: $20.91

Payment:
□ Check
□ Credit card: □ MasterCard □ VISA
Card number: _____
Name on card: _____
Expiration date: _____
Ship to:
Name: _____
Address: _____
City, State and Zip _____
Phone number (   ) _____

Voices of Michigan may also be purchased at your local bookstore.